THE COMPLETE

Fish & Shellfish

COOKBOOK

OVER 200 DELICIOUSLY DIVERSE RECIPES FROM THE
WORLD'S FINEST CUISINES

THE COMPLETE

Fish & Shellfish

C O O K B O O K

OVER 200 DELICIOUSLY DIVERSE RECIPES FROM THE
WORLD'S FINEST CUISINES

EDITED BY DIANA VOWLES

CHARTWELL
BOOKS, INC.

A QUINTET BOOK

Published in 2004 by Chartwell Books
A Division of Book Sales, Inc.
114 Northfield Avenue
New Jersey 08837

This edition produced for sale in the U.S.A.,
its territories and dependencies only.

ISBN 0-7858-1845-6

This book was designed and produced by
Quintet Publishing Limited
6 Blundell Street
London N7 9BH

Creative Director: Richard Dewing
Designer: Stuart Walden
Project Editor: Stefanie Foster

Typeset in Great Britain by
Central Southern Typesetters, Eastbourne
Manufactured by Bright Art (Singapore) Pte Ltd
Printed in Singapore by
Star Standard Industries Pte Ltd

Contents

Introduction

M ☐☐☐☐☐☐ Microwave dishes are indicated by this symbol next to the recipe title.

It is always fascinating to see that many people will eat fish dishes in restaurants, yet rarely will they prepare the same simple fare at home. Fish is very often best cooked without frills, by broiling, baking or poaching, and no one does more preparation for the consumer than the fish merchant! There is very little waste as the bones and heads can be used to make fish stock. It is often the thought of making these stocks that makes fish cooking seem complicated. In fact, they are the work of minutes and greatly enhance the delicate flavor of the fish when cooked; it is generally much quicker to cook fish than meat.

Nowadays there is such a variety of fish available that the choice can be bewildering and many cooks tend to stick to the familiar few. However, with a little experiment, great variety can be added to everyday menus. Excellent freezing techniques have made it possible to buy a great selection. Fish is often frozen at sea and therefore extremely fresh if properly stored and thawed.

More expensive fish, such as salmon, turbot and halibut, are excellent value for money because, being rich, large portions are unnecessary. Shellfish are extremely versatile, highly nutritious and amazingly simple to prepare if you are a novice fish cook. Ask the staff at your fish merchant's or the supermarket's fish counter for advice and they will usually do all the groundwork for you.

Fish is an excellent source of protein and, as most people are conscious of healthy eating, it is comforting to know that the fat content of fish is largely unsaturated. This means fish, as long as it is not fried, can play a valuable part in providing the protein we need without adding to the cholesterol levels which are associated with heart disease.

The nutrient content of most fish is made up as follows: 25% protein; 22% fats; 2% minerals and 85% water. White fish have very little fat in the flesh, about 0.5%, and in some fish, such as haddock and cod, the fat is laid down in the liver. This makes the flesh of white fish particularly valuable in lowfat diets. Because the fat is mainly unsaturated, even the oily fish, such as mackerel and herring, are wonderful sources of high-energy food. Recent research suggests that fish oils can help to break down cholesterol in the body. Fish and fish oils are a rich source of vitamins A and D which we all need for glowing health.

The ideal slimmer's food usually contains very little carbohydrate and this makes fish suitable for diets. However, calorie counters must sacrifice all those delicious buttery sauces and settle instead for poaching and baking with the addition of lemon juice and fresh herbs. Mind you, this is not such a sacrifice for the end result will be just as tasty. Those on gluten-free and diabetic diets can also enjoy fish provided that no flour products are used in their preparation.

The fish used for recipes in this book are often interchangeable with other similar types of fish. Although classic recipes may seem forbidding they have been simplified where possible and many popular favorites which are becoming "little classics" have been included, especially in the section for appetizers.

Fish appetizers are so popular now for entertaining that fish as a main course is often overlooked, which is a pity. Fish can be ideal as a party main course or the focus of the buffet table. Its delicacy should always be remembered when choosing vegetables and wine.

Strong flavors can spoil the taste of the fish. Tomatoes, mushrooms, peas, green beans, broccoli, carrots, leeks and potatoes are all good basic vegetables to serve. Rice with onion, chopped tomato and chopped pepper is delicious, too, with fish dishes which have a sauce, but rice and fish without a sauce can be rather dry and uninteresting.

The sauce section in the book is important, as many simple dishes have classic sauces served with them and it is these that turn the meal into a feast.

Fish is nutritious and priced competitively in comparison with other high-protein foods, and enables you to produce gourmet meals surprisingly quickly. There is no reason at all for people to feel unsure of their abilities to cook any variety of fish dishes.

SELECTION

When you are buying fish and shellfish, bear in mind that absolute freshness is essential. Look for bright eyes and stiff flesh, which are the signs of fresh fish. Dull eyes and limp flesh with a slight ammonia smell indicate stale fish.

It is best to buy fish the day it is to be cooked. Store it loosely covered in the refrigerator and, if you cannot eat it the same day, try not to keep it longer than 24 hours before cooking.

PREPARATION OF FISH

Ideally, fish should be prepared just before cooking but time does not always permit this. If it is to be cooked in a stock it is often advantageous to allow it to cool in the fish liquid.

Most people are not keen on cleaning or gutting fish and it is fortunate that fish merchants are so helpful with preparation.

However, for those who are prepared to do the work themselves, this is how it should be done.

To scale fish, lay the fish on a piece of paper towel and hold the fish by the tail. Always scrape the scales from the tail toward the head, using the blunt side of a knife. Rinse under cold water.

To clean and fillet flat fish

1 *Slit behind the head on the dark skin side, remove the entrails and rinse in cold water. Pat dry with paper towels. Remove the fins with a knife or scissors. Begin filleting by cutting into the head end against the bone.*

3 *Turn the fish over, insert the knife at the head and carefully remove the second fillet in the same way. The flat fish is now filleted. One fillet has thick black skin, the other white skin. The bone can now be used for fish stock (see page 18).*

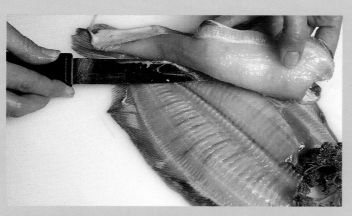

2 *Cut the fillet away carefully with the skin attached to it, leaving the bone as clean as possible.*

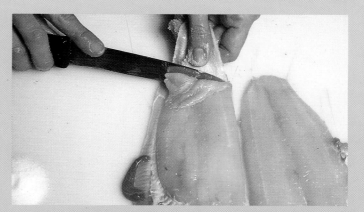

4 *To skin the fish, hold the tail firmly and work the flesh away from the skin from tail to head-end, using a sharp knife. The skin can also be used for fish stock.*

1 *If the head is not required for stock, such as with mackerel and herring, cut it off with a sharp knife before boning.*

2 *To clean retaining the head, slit from under the head down to the tail.*

3 *Remove the entrails by hooking your finger under the throat and pulling down toward the tail. Wash well. A rubber glove may be used for this step.*

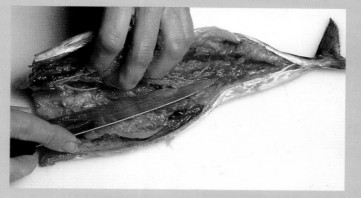

4 *Slip the sharp knife under the bone on each side of the fish then open the fish and remove the bone.*

5 *An alternative method which may be easier for the inexperienced is to turn the fish open-side downward. Press down on the back with the heel of your hand to loosen the bone.*

6 *Turn the fish over and, starting at the tail end, place the blade of the knife under the bone and push along the spine to release. Feel the surface of the fish with your fingers to ensure there are no stray bones. The round fish is now ready to be cooked.*

Methods of Cooking Fish

BAKING

This method of cooking uses a controlled temperature in an oven. When fat or oil is used the food is said to be roasted. Baking in the oven is suitable for whole fish and some fish fillets.

Foil and casseroles are often used for baking fish in. Baking ensures an even distribution of heat for the complete cooking of fish, or the first stage of a fish dish, which may have a delicious sauce made from the juices left over from the cooking in the oven.

Most whole fish are baked at 350°F. Smaller fish or fillets are usually cooked at around 400°F for a shorter time (see individual recipes).

Fish should be brushed with a little fat or oil, and usually some liquid such as Court-Bouillon (see page 19) or wine flavored with herbs is also added.

BRAISING OR CASSEROLING

This method can be carried out either on top of the stove or in the oven and will include a selection of vegetables, stock or wine with the fish which is cooked in a casserole or baking dish.

Remember that the vegetable must be tender at the same time as the fish is cooked. Therefore, it is usually advisable to sweat the vegetables first (by cooking over a low heat) to make sure that they are partially cooked before adding the fish.

Large chunks of fish, fish steaks and cutlets can all be cooked by this method.

MICROWAVE COOKING

The microwave oven cooks fish very successfully, retaining all the natural moisture and delicacy – and, needless to say, it is very quick. It is also an excellent way to reheat dishes to avoid any loss of texture and flavor.

It is usually advisable to cook fish covered with plastic wrap which has had slits cut in it. Place the thinner ends of the fish toward the middle of the dish, overlapping them if necessary.

To cook fish which requires flaking in a recipe, cook it until it is just firm and then leave it to stand for a few minutes. It will then flake quite easily.

Brush fish which has the skin left on, such as trout, with butter, otherwise no fat is necessary. If sauce is to be added to the fish in the microwave, it is usually advisable to do this halfway through the cooking process.

Cooking fish fillets takes approximately 9–10 minutes per 1 lb. at 500 watts; 7–8 minutes per 1 lb. at 600 watts; 6–7 minutes per 1 lb. at 650 watts. Whole fish will take approximately 11–13 minutes per 1 lb. at 500 watts; 8–10 minutes per 1 lb. at 600 watts; 7–9 minutes per 1 lb. at 650 watts.

DEEP-FRYING

Although many people try to cut down on fried food, this is one of the most traditional and delicious ways to eat some types of fish. It is especially suited to small fish, such as sprats, and fish fillets, and it is a popular way to cook shrimp.

The fish must be evenly coated before frying to provide a crisp outside and to prevent the fish breaking up and the fat soaking through into the flesh.

Preheat the fat to 325°–375°F, depending on the size of the fish. It is essential to have hot oil to seal the coating and prevent soggy, oily fish. To test for correct frying temperature without a thermostat, use a cube of stale bread: drop it into the fat and it should rise to the surface crisp and evenly browned in 1 minute if the temperature is correct. There are many safe and useful electric deep-fat friers available with temperature controls which remove the guesswork from frying.

If using a deep saucepan with a basket, take care to avoid accidents. The pan should be filled less than two-thirds full. Do not let flames "lick" up the sides of the pan. If an accident does occur and the fat catches fire, do not use water to douse the flames. Instead cover immediately with a metal lid to exclude the air and turn off the heat immediately. Do not uncover until the flame dies down.

POACHING

This method involves cooking gently in liquid. It is most often used for whole fish fillets and steaks.

Place the liquid in a skillet or saucepan as large as the fish. Milk, stock, water or wine can all be used according to the recipe, usually with herbs and other seasonings. Place the prepared fish in the pan; whole fillets, such as smoked haddock, can be topped with small knobs of butter.

Poaching is done over a low heat. If the liquid is allowed to boil, the fish will lose its delicate taste and texture. The liquid left over from poaching can be used as liquid in a sauce to accompany the fish.

STEAMING

This method of cooking fish makes it light and easy to digest. It is an excellent way to cook food for babies, convalescents and anyone with a digestive problem, or anyone on a light diet.

Fillets can be rolled or placed flat between two plates over steadily simmering water. Otherwise use a steamer or a pressure cooker. Follow the manufacturer's directions for best results when using the latter.

SHALLOW-FRYING

Shallow frying, which is sometimes known as sautéing or pan-frying, covers the method of cooking the fish in a skillet in a shallow layer of oil or fat.

Coat the fish in either flour or egg and crumbs, as in deep-frying. The fish will require turning and looking after constantly to obtain an even golden-brown and crisp appearance.

BROILING

This is a fast method of cooking fillets of fish, fish steaks, cutlets and small whole fish. To save extra dish washing, it is advisable to line the broiler pan with foil and, to prevent the fish sticking to the wire rack, brush with oil before starting to cook.

Preheat the broiler and brush the fish with melted butter or oil. Whole fish should have several cuts made in the skin to allow the heat to penetrate evenly.

Season the fish and place under the broiler. After 1 minute, lower the heat to medium. Most average-sized fish or cutlets will take 8–10 minutes.

EN PAPILLOTE

This means cooking food in a paper case in the oven. It is especially good for whole fish and steaks because all the goodness and flavor are sealed in the paper packages. The added advantage is that there is no messy pan to clean.

It is an ideal method of cooking for slimmers as the fish is simply sprinkled with lemon juice, herbs and other seasonings and cooked in its own juice.

The fish can be enclosed in a buttered piece of waxed parchment paper, although most people use foil for "package" cooking now.

Sauces and butters

A good sauce can be the making of a fish dish, complementing natural flavors and bringing added interest to a meal. Simpler still, a savory herb butter can be stored in the freezer and thawed when needed — serve with broiled or fried fish instead of a sauce, or beat into a sauce or soup.

While you will find a recipe to suit every occasion in this book, do not be afraid to branch out and create your own recipes by trying different combinations of fishes and flavors — the classic sauces have gained their place in the hall of fame by being versatile!

Béchamel Sauce

[MAKES 2½ CUPS SAUCE]

A good béchamel sauce enhances any dish requiring a white sauce and is well worth the extra few minutes it takes to prepare. In some fish dishes the liquid in which the fish has been baked or poached is substituted for half or all of the milk. Sauce made with a stock or stock and wine is known as a velouté sauce.

2½ cups milk	3 tbsp. butter, depending
I small peeled onion, quartered	on thickness required
I bay leaf	½ cup all-purpose flour, depending
a few peppercorns	on
I blade of mace	thickness required
I parsley stem	salt and white pepper

1 Place the milk in a saucepan with the onion, bay leaf, peppercorns, mace and parsley. Cover and let heat up on a low heat for about 10 minutes without boiling. Remove from the heat and leave to stand for a further 10 minutes, covered. Strain and set aside.

2 Make the roux (a liaison of butter and flour) by melting the butter in a saucepan – do not brown. Add the flour and mix well over a low heat.

3 Gradually add the strained milk and continue stirring until creamy and thick. Season to taste.

FISH STOCK

To make a good fish stock, add fish trimmings to the Court-Bouillon opposite, leaving out the vinegar. The vegetables should not be simmered for longer than 30 minutes, or the stock will become bitter.

Note 1 *After fish has been cooked in the Court-Bouillon, the liquid becomes a fish stock.*

Note 2 *To make* **fish glaze***, reduce the stock until it reaches a thick, syrupy consistency.*

Hollandaise Sauce

[MAKES 1¼ CUPS]

Hollandaise is served hot with broiled fish such as salmon, turbot, halibut and sea bream. Make the sauce in a double boiler or an ovenproof bowl over a saucepan of simmering water. If using the latter method, make sure that the bottom of the bowl is not touching the hot water or the sauce will set on the bottom of the bowl before it is cooked.

2 tbsp. water	2 egg yolks
6 peppercorns, slightly crushed	I tbsp. lemon juice
I tbsp. white-wine vinegar	salt to taste
¾ cup butter	

1 Place the water, crushed peppercorns and white-wine vinegar in a small saucepan and reduce to about 1 tbsp. liquid. Set aside.

2 Cut the butter into pieces and soften gently in a small saucepan. Remove from the heat.

3 Beat the egg yolks, reduced liquid and a little of the butter in the double boiler. When the mixture becomes creamy and slightly thick, pour in the remaining butter in a thin stream, beating briskly. Add lemon juice and a little salt, and taste for seasoning.

4 Remove from the heat as soon as it is thick. If the sauce looks as if it is curdling, add a few drops of cold water and beat briskly for a few more minutes. This sauce can be made in a blender or food processor, but you may find that less butter will be absorbed. The addition of 1 tbsp. cold water with the lemon juice will prevent the sauce from becoming too thick.

BEARNAISE SAUCE

Add another teaspoon of vinegar and some tarragon to the first ingredients for Hollandaise Sauce before reducing. The flavor of béarnaise sauce is altogether more piquant and the end result should be slightly thicker than hollandaise with 1 tbsp. chopped tarragon and 1 tbsp. chopped chervil added. If these are unobtainable, use 2 tsp. dried tarragon and 1 tbsp. fresh chopped parsley.

MOUSSELINE SAUCE

Add 4 tbsp. whipped cream to the Hollandaise Sauce as it cools and the resulting mousseline sauce can be served cold with fish or vegetables.

Court-Bouillon

[TO COOK I LB. FISH]

This is used for cooking salmon, trout, crayfish and lobster. It can be used several times if strained each time.

6 cups water	**I oz. parsley stems**
2 tsp. salt	**4 tbsp. white wine or white**
3 cups peeled and	**wine vinegar**
sliced carrots	**2 bouquets garnis or 2 bay leaves**
3 cups peeled and	**sprigs of thyme**
sliced onions	**6 peppercorns, slightly crushed**

I Place all the ingredients, except the peppercorns, in a fish kettle or large saucepan. Bring the liquid to a boil and skim.

2 Simmer for approximately 3–5 minutes then add the crushed peppercorns. Continue simmering for a further 10–20 minutes. Leave to cool and strain through a fine strainer.

3 To store, pour into a plastic bag set in a bowl or plastic box and freeze until cooking fish again. The bag may be taken out and sealed when frozen.

Mayonnaise

[MAKES APPROXIMATELY 1 ¼ CUPS]

2 egg yolks
1 ¼ cups vegetable or olive oil
½ tsp salt
pinch of white pepper

pinch of dried mustard
1 tbsp. white-wine vinegar or
lemon juice

1 Use the eggs at room temperature, not directly from the refrigerator. Place the yolks in a *slightly* warmed but dry bowl. Mix for a few seconds.

2 Gradually add the oil a few drops at a time, beating constantly with a wooden spoon or a small wire whisk. The mixture will become a thick, creamy emulsion after a little oil is added. Continue to beat in the rest of the oil gradually.

3 Mix the rest of the ingredients together and add a few drops at a time when the mixture becomes thick; this will make the sauce thinner. Taste for seasoning.

AÏOLI

Soak 1 slice of bread in a little milk, or use 1 small mashed potato.

Crush 2–4 cloves of garlic depending on taste and mix with the squeezed bread or potato. Make a paste, then add only 1 egg yolk to the mixture.

Proceed as for mayonnaise but add 1–2 tbsp. boiled warm water when the mixture becomes thick.

Serve with broiled and cold fish and shellfish. It is also served with Provençal fish soups.

SAUCE GRIBICHE

Add the strained yolk of a hard-boiled egg, ½ tsp. Dijon mustard, 1 tbsp. chopped pickled gherkins, 1 tsp. fresh tarragon or ½ tsp. dried, 1 tbsp. freshly chopped parsley and 1 tsp. chopped capers to 1 ¼ cups mayonnaise. The egg white, cut into very thin strips, may be added before serving. Serve with cold fish dishes and shellfish.

GREEN SAUCE

Purée 1 bunch of washed watercress with stems removed with 2 oz. cooked and well-drained fresh or frozen spinach, a few sprigs of parsley and 2 tsp. fresh tarragon or 1 tsp. dried, and add to the mayonnaise. This is delicious served with cold fish dishes.

SEAFOOD SAUCE

Add ⅔ cup whipped cream with 2 tsp. brandy added and a few drops of hot-pepper sauce to 1 ¼ cups well-flavored mayonnaise.

Note *All these sauces can be made in a blender or food processor. Use the whole egg when making this type of uncooked sauce in a machine. The advantage is that the machine produces a finer emulsion which keeps longer than the handmade variety, and only takes a few seconds to make.*

If using chilled mayonnaise-type sauces, allow them to return to room temperature before stirring to avoid separation.

To rescue what is commonly known as "curdled mayonnaise" (this can happen if the oil is added too fast or the ingredients are too cold), start again with another egg yolk, a pinch of mustard and a few drops of hot water. Put the mixture in a clean warm bowl and add the curdled sauce, one spoonful at a time, beating briskly. When the sauce becomes an emulsion again, add the remainder of the curdled sauce gradually, beating until a thick creamy mixture is made. Taste for seasoning.

Mornay Sauce

[MAKES APPROXIMATELY 2½ CUPS]

This can be served with poached or steamed fillets or cutlets.

2½ cups Béchamel Sauce (see page 18) 2 egg yolks	¼ cup heavy cream ⅓ cup grated cheese

1 Place 4 tbsp. Béchamel Sauce in a small bowl and mix with the egg yolks and cream.

2 Add this mixture to the remaining Béchamel Sauce and cook over a low heat, stirring well.

3 Gradually add the grated cheese. Parmesan cheese is ideal but individual taste can decide on the type of cheese.

Chaudfroid Sauce

[MAKES 2½ CUPS]

2 cups Béchamel Sauce (see page 18) ⅔ cup liquid aspic	1 rounded tsp. gelatin 2 tbsp. boiling water

1 Allow the Béchamel Sauce to cool but cover with plastic wrap to avoid a skin forming.

2 Make up the liquid aspic in a measuring jug and sprinkle the gelatin onto the hot water. Make sure the mixture is dissolved by placing the measuring jug in a saucepan of boiling water. Leave to cool before using to coat fish fillets, small fish or steaks.

Beurre Blanc

[SERVES 4]

Beurre blanc is another sauce that strikes terror into the amateur heart. If you follow the directions patiently, you will not fail. Your sauce should achieve the consistency of thick cream. If too thick, beat a little more over low heat. If too thin – and unmelted – cool a little.
As to the fish, salmon or anything freshwater, poached.

2 cups dry white wine	salt and pepper to taste
⅔ cup white-wine vinegar	2 cups butter
1 medium onion, very finely chopped	

1 Combine the white wine and the wine vinegar. Set the wine, vinegar and onion over a very high heat and reduce until almost nothing remains. (This is literally true: the pan should contain nothing more than a shiny coating.)

2 As the wine mixture reduces, work a little salt and pepper into the butter.

3 Now employ an intermittent low heat: 30 seconds on, 30 seconds off. Using this technique, slowly beat the butter into the reduced wine mixture. (Beat constantly with a whisk so the butter stays creamy. It must not melt.)

Mustard Sauce

[MAKES ⅔ CUP]

1 tbsp. French mustard	salt and white pepper
juice of ½ lemon	⅔ cup whipping cream

1 Mix the mustard, lemon juice and seasoning together.

2 Whip the cream lightly and stir in the mustard mixture. Chill before using with broiled or fried fish.

VARIATION

Alternatively, a hot mustard sauce may be made with ⅔ cup Béchamel Sauce (see page 18). Add 1 tsp. dried mustard and 1 tsp. vinegar to 1 tbsp. of the sauce, return to the sauce and stir over the heat for a further minute.

Red Wine, Mushroom and Onion Sauce, Mâcon Style

[SERVES 6]

*You can use this sauce for trout, either whole or in fillets if it's a big
sea trout, sole, salmon and tuna. Bonito and snapper would fare equally
well, as would any well-fleshed river fish.*

2 cups dry red wine
¾ cup butter
18 or so pearl onions, peeled
salt to taste

a pinch of sugar
3 cups mushrooms
2 tbsp. all-purpose flour

1 Poach the fish in the red wine. Set aside and reserve the wine.

2 Melt ¼ cup of the butter over a medium heat and stir in the onions.
Add salt to taste and the sugar.

3 Just cover the onions with water and simmer until the liquid has
evaporated – about 10 minutes – and the onions are agreeably glazed.
Set aside.

4 Sauté the mushrooms in ¼ cup butter. Set aside.

5 Place the reserved wine from the fish on a high heat and reduce
by half.

6 Mix the remaining butter with the flour and beat into the wine on
a low heat. Combine the wine mixture with the onions and
mushrooms and bring the mixture to the boil.

7 Arrange the fish on a suitable dish, pour the sauce over it
and serve.

Tomato Sauce

[MAKES APPROXIMATELY 2½ CUPS]

2 tbsp. oil
I large onion, peeled and diced
I–2 cloves garlic, crushed
I celery stick, scrubbed
I carrot, scraped and grated
14-oz. can tomatoes
3 cups skinned and chopped
fresh tomatoes
I bouquet garni

2 bay leaves
I tbsp. chopped fresh basil,
or I tsp. dried basil
parsley sprig
½ tsp. sugar
salt and freshly ground
black pepper
I¼ cups fish or chicken stock
2 tbsp. red wine

1 Heat the oil in a saucepan. Cook the onion and garlic over a low heat for about 4 minutes until transparent.

2 Remove the strings from the celery stick and chop into small pieces, then add to the onion and garlic for the last 2 minutes.

3 Add all the other ingredients, bring to a boil and simmer for 40 minutes on a low heat.

4 Remove the parsley, bay leaf and bouquet garni and serve as cooked, or partially blend if you prefer a smoother texture.

Tartar Sauce

[MAKES 1¼ CUPS]

Serve with all types of fried or broiled fish.

2 hard-boiled eggs
2 tsp. French mustard
salt and freshly ground pepper
I egg yolk
⅔ cup vegetable or olive oil

4–6 pickled gherkins
2 tbsp. capers
2 tbsp. finely chopped fresh
parsley
I tsp. dried chervil or fresh
if available

1 Push the yolks of the hard-boiled eggs through a fine mesh strainer into a bowl and add mustard, salt and pepper.

2 Mix the raw egg yolk into the bowl and cream until the mixture is a smooth paste.

3 Add the oil a few drops at a time until the sauce is thick. If it seems too thick add a few drops of lemon juice.

4 Drain and rinse the pickled gherkins and capers in a strainer under the cold tap as they are usually packed in vinegar or brine, which can overpower the flavor of the sauce. Pat dry with paper towels then chop finely.

5 Add to the sauce with the herbs (the herbs, gherkins and capers can be chopped in the blender or food processor). Mix well and taste for seasoning.

QUICK TARTAR SAUCE

Add the pickled gherkins, capers, parsley and herbs to ⅔ cup mayonnaise.

Tartar Sauce ▶

Spicy Tomato Sauce

[MAKES ABOUT 2 CUPS]

2 tbsp. oil
I large onion, peeled and chopped
I green pepper, seeded and finely diced
I red pepper, seeded and finely diced
I green chili pepper, seeded and finely chopped
14 oz. can tomatoes
2 fresh tomatoes, peeled and chopped

¼ tsp. dried mustard
salt and freshly ground pepper
I bouquet garni
2 bay leaves
¼ tsp. sugar
⅔ cup fish or chicken stock
I green chili, seeded and finely chopped, to garnish

1 Heat the oil in a saucepan and sweat the onion on a low heat until transparent. Add the peppers and chili to the onions and cook on a low heat for about 4 minutes.

2 Add the rest of the ingredients to the onion and pepper mixture. Bring to a boil, reduce the heat and simmer for 30 minutes. Remove the bouquet garni and bay leaves.

3 The sauce may be partially blended if liked. Serve with chopped green chili on top.

Mussel and Shrimp Sauce, Dieppe Style

[SERVES 6]

This is a light but chunky sauce. You could use it with any poached or broiled flat fish such as Dover sole or turbot to emphasize their luxury. It is not a sauce for anything oily.

Mussel-cooking liquid is easily obtained: simply sweat the mussels in a closed pan and collect the juices that flow after they have opened. If the liquid is short, add a drop of water or white wine.

⅔ cup dry white wine
⅔ cup mussel cooking liquid
2½ cups White Wine Velouté
Sauce (page 18)

¼ cup butter
¼ lb. cooked mussels
¼ lb. cooked and shelled
shrimp

1 Mix together the white wine and the mussel liquid. Set on a high heat and boil hard to reduce the volume by one-half.

2 Remove from the heat and beat in the butter.

3 Add the velouté, the mussels and the shrimp and reheat briefly.

Maitre d'Hotel Butter

*It is usual to make up herb butters in the shape of a thick link sausage.
Wrap the butter in foil and cut slices as required after chilling. It is
convenient to make up several flavors. Cut the rolls into coin-sized
pieces when very cold and store in the freezer.*

¼ cup butter, softened	**salt and freshly ground pepper**
2 tsp. lemon juice	**I tbsp. chopped fresh parsley**

I Cream all the ingredients together, chill and use on broiled food.

Lemon-Tarragon Butter

¼ cup butter, softened	**I tbsp. chopped fresh tarragon,**
juice of ½ lemon	**or I tsp. dried**
salt and pepper	

I Cream all the ingredients together and chill.

Garlic Butter

¼ cup butter, softened	**2 tsp. chopped fresh parsley**
I–2 cloves garlic, crushed	**(optional)**

I Cream the butter and add the garlic. Blend well. Parsley is optional
but gives a better flavor to the butter. Chill well.

Brown Butter and Lemon Sauce

[SERVES 4]

½ cup butter	a little chopped fresh parsley
juice of ½ lemon	

1 Melt the butter in a skillet over a high heat. Allow it to foam, then watch carefully until it begins to brown.

2 Take the butter off the heat, toss in the lemon juice and allow the sizzle to subside a little. (Otherwise the butter will spit all over.)

3 Pour the mixture over the fish and sprinkle the parsley on top. *Picture on page 16.*

Anchovy Butter

6 anchovy fillets	pepper
2 tbsp. milk	1 drop hot-pepper sauce
6 tbsp. butter	

1 Soak all the anchovy fillets in milk. Mash in a bowl with a wooden spoon until creamy. Cream all the ingredients together and chill.

Mustard Butter

¼ cup butter, softened	salt and pepper
1 tbsp. French mustard	

1 Cream all the ingredients together and chill.

Green Butter

It is simple to make this excellent savory butter in a blender or food processor, otherwise all ingredients have to be chopped by hand.

2 oz. spinach leaves, washed	3 pickled gherkins
1 bunch of watercress,	1 tsp. capers
stems removed	3 anchovy fillets
1 clove garlic	2 tbsp. oil
fresh tarragon, to taste	1 egg yolk
a few sprigs of parsley	1 hard-boiled egg
fresh chives, to taste	½ cup butter, softened

1 Purée the spinach leaves, watercress, garlic and herbs. Add the pickled gherkins, capers and anchovy fillets with the oil, egg yolk and hard-boiled egg. Lastly blend in the softened butter.

2 Chill and serve with broiled or barbecued fish. This savory butter is especially good with barbecued food.

Soups and appetizers

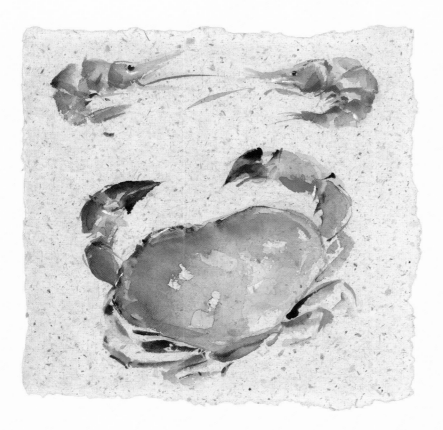

*While once the range of fish appetizers might have been quite limited,
a more international outlook has brought many new delights to our
tables. Old favorites, such as Smoked Mackerel Pâté and Shrimp Bisque,
are joined in this chapter by the classic Provençal Fish Soup and Moules
à la Marinière from France, Herring Salad from Germany and
Oysters Rockefeller.*

Shrimp Bisque

[SERVES 6]

The soup should need no salt. If you have saved a few whole, shelled
shrimp for a garnish, so much the better.
You might find it a bore to save shrimp shells. Instead make the broth
when you eat the shrimp and reduce it by boiling to a manageable size,
then freeze it until you want to make this bisque.

I lb. shrimp shells
(*see* Brochette of Shrimp,
page 141)
6¼ cup water
5 tbsp. butter
I small carrot
I medium onion, very finely
chopped

I bay leaf
4 tbsp. chopped fresh parsley
¼ cup brandy
½ cup all-purpose flour
5 tbsp. tomato paste
⅔ cup heavy cream

I Boil the shrimp shells in the water for 1 hour.

2 In the meanwhile, melt the butter in a large saucepan over a low heat. Add the carrot, onion, bay leaf and parsley, and stew very gently for about 10 minutes. Add the brandy and remove from the heat.

3 After 1 hour, strain the shrimp shells and top up the broth with water up to a quantity of 5 cups.

4 Add the flour to the butter, vegetables and brandy mixture and cook gently for 3–4 minutes. Slowly add the shell broth and bring the liquid to a boil.

5 Add the tomato paste, then purée the mixture or force through a fine strainer. Return the mixture to the heat, beat in the cream and serve immediately.

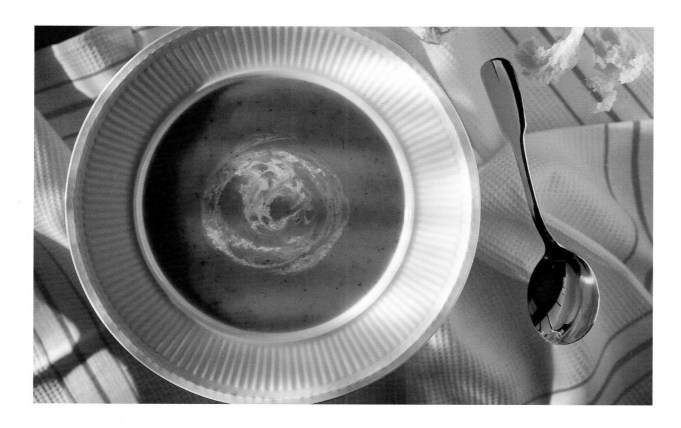

Provençal Fish Soup

[SERVES 6]

This soup is traditionally served with three accompaniments which are among the most inspired in the French kitchen. They are: rouille, a mayonnaise strongly flavored with cayenne pepper and garlic and colored with paprika; toasted French bread; grated Gruyère cheese.

1 lb. white fish trimmings
1 large onion, peeled and halved
2 tbsp. chopped fresh parsley
2 bay leaves
juice of 1 lemon
2½ quarts water

10 white peppercorns
¾ cup tomato paste
2 tbsp. paprika
1 pinch saffron or turmeric
salt and pepper to taste

1 Put the fish, onion, parsley, bay leaves and lemon juice into the water and bring to a boil. Turn down the heat and simmer gently for 25–30 minutes.

2 Add the peppercorns and let the broth stand for 5 minutes or so. Strain, discard all the debris and replace the broth on a high heat.

3 Add the tomato paste, paprika and saffron or turmeric. Reduce the broth by one-third. Season to taste with salt and pepper. This soup can be made ahead and reheated – this also gives the flavors time to combine and mature.

Salad of Baby Squid with Oil, Garlic and Chili Peppers

[SERVES 4–6]

Use a large volume of water so that the heat given off, as well as its temperature, remains high.
The heat is essential because you need to cook the squid very quickly.
Lemon juice is added to whiten the flesh. Do this with any poached fish, if whiteness takes your fancy.

2 lb. baby squid	3 green chili peppers,
juice of 1 lemon	sliced and seeded
1¼ cups olive oil	salt and freshly ground black
6 medium cloves garlic, sliced	pepper

1 Clean the squid (see page 165) and slice the bodies into rings.

2 Bring at least 4 times the volume of water as you have squid to a brisk boil. Add the lemon juice.

3 Plunge the prepared squid into the boiling water and cook until the flesh loses its translucency. This will take no longer than 1 minute. Immediately remove the squid from the pan and plunge it into cold water to stop the cooking process.

4 In a separate saucepan, heat the olive oil until 1 piece of garlic sizzles fiercely when dropped in. Add all the garlic. Cook at a high heat for 30 seconds or so, then remove from the heat. The garlic will continue to cook.

5 When the garlic pieces have turned mid-brown, add the sliced chili and return the pan to the heat for a further 30 seconds.

6 Remove the pan from the heat and leave the cooking to continue. Both garlic and chili should now be dark brown and crunchy.

7 Allow the oil, garlic and chili to cool before you dress the seasoned squid with it.

Fish Soup

[SERVES 8–10]

Deliciously light and savory, this Russian fish soup is traditionally made during the summer and fall months.

2 quarts water	½ cup heavy cream
2 medium onions, finely chopped	1 cup white wine
2 tsp. finely chopped fresh parsley	¼ tsp. white pepper
¼ tsp. finely grated lemon peel	1 garlic clove, crushed
1 bay leaf	2 large cucumbers, peeled and cut
¼ tsp. black pepper	into slices
1 lb. halibut cutlets,	1 lb. tomatoes, peeled,
cut into pieces	seeded and cut into pieces
1 lb. swordfish cutlets,	½ cup pitted and halved
cut into pieces	ripe olives

1 In a very large stockpot, combine the water, onions, parsley, lemon peel, bay leaf and black pepper. Bring the liquid to a boil, reduce the heat and simmer for 2 minutes.

2 Add the fish to the pot and simmer for 5 minutes. Reduce the heat to low and simmer for a further 5 minutes.

3 Add the cream, white wine, white pepper, garlic clove, cucumbers and tomatoes to the pot. Simmer over a low heat for 5 minutes. Do not let the soup boil.

4 Remove the pot from the heat. Stir in the olives. Leave the soup to stand for 30 seconds. Stir again and serve.

German Herring Salad

[SERVES 6]

This piquant herring salad is a delicious way to start a meal. Serve it on a bed of lettuce with thin slices of crusty bread.

14 oz.–1 lb. herring fillets	2 tbsp. olive oil
½ cup diced cooked beet	¼ cup lemon juice
3 scallions (including tops), diced	½ tsp. black pepper
2 tbsp. white-wine vinegar	¼ cup orange juice
½ tsp. dried tarragon	1 tbsp. Dijon-style mustard
½ tsp. dried dill	

1 Combine all the ingredients in a blender or food processor and chop finely. Spoon the salad into a serving bowl, cover tightly and refrigerate for at least 1 hour before serving.

Scallop and Snow Pea Salad

[SERVES 4]

Frozen scallops can be used if fresh ones cannot be had. Try to get them frozen with the coral – it is frequently absent from frozen packs.

**12 fresh scallops
½ lb. snow peas,
topped and tailed
1 tbsp. fresh chopped mint
French Dressing (see page 143)**

**handful of lamb's lettuce,
washed and drained
1 tbsp. lemon juice
2 tbsp. very small fried croutons**

1 Clean the scallops, saving any juices and removing the muscular white frill found opposite the orange coral. Rinse off any black matter. Separate the corals from the body. Slice the white part of the scallops into 2 or 3 horizontally, but leave the corals whole.

2 Blanch (put into a saucepan of boiling salted water) the snow peas for 3–4 minutes. Refresh (run under cold water until cold) to prevent further cooking and set the color. Drain well.

3 Add the mint to the French Dressing, and in it toss together the snow peas and lamb's lettuce. Place on 4 side plates.

4 Put the scallops into a pan with the lemon juice and their own juices. Put on a well-fitting lid and gently shake and toss them over a moderate heat for 30 seconds, or until they have lost their glassiness and become very slightly firmer to the touch.

5 Tip the warm scallops and the juices over the snow peas, scatter on the croutons and serve immediately.

Smoked Mackerel Pâté

[SERVES 4]

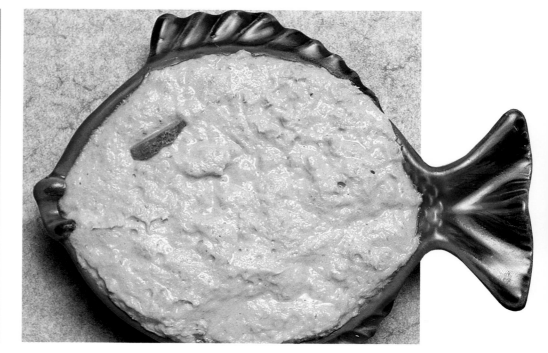

This makes a very firm pâté – you can make a softer mixture by adding more yogurt. It then makes a dip for serving with carrot and other vegetable sticks etc. This freezes very well.

**½ lb. smoked mackerel fillets
⅔ cup plain yogurt
2 tsp. grated horseradish**

**1 tbsp. lemon juice
salt and pepper**

1 Skin the fish and remove any bones. Purée all the ingredients together. Spoon into individual dishes or one serving dish. Refrigerate until required.

Salmon Mousse Chaudfroid

[SERVES 4]

If your chaudfroid sauce won't set and your quantities were correct, then the mousse was not cold enough, the chaudfroid was not lukewarm, or the layers were too thick, or all three.
Remember to season highly to avoid blandness. All seasoning loses its strength (as transmitted through the tastebuds) when it is chilled. Under-seasoning therefore results in undesirable blandness.

¾ lb. skinned and boned fresh salmon
1¼ cups heavy cream
12 sprigs of fresh dill or basil
salt and coarsely ground black pepper
cayenne pepper

1¼ cups Fish Velouté Sauce, *or* 1¼ cups Béchamel Sauce (page 18)
⅔ cup stiff aspic jelly
¼ cup butter
leaf of basil or sprig of dill, to garnish

1 Mash the salmon meat as finely as you can. (Use a blender or food processor, if available.) It should be entirely paste-like. Whip the cream and fold it into the salmon.

2 Finely chop half the basil or dill, add to the mixture and season highly with the salt, black pepper and cayenne. Taste it for yourself to assess seasoning; the mixture is perfectly edible even raw.

3 Coat 4 ramekins with the melted butter and force the fish mixture well down into each.

4 Set the ramekins in a skillet on top of the stove. Fill the pan with boiling water to within ½ in. of the top of the ramekins and cover the whole pan well.

5 Poach very gently – the water must not bubble over into the fish – for 12–15 minutes. It will be cooked when the mixture shrinks away from the sides of the pot.

6 Remove the mousses from the ramekins and set aside to chill.

7 Heat the Velouté or Béchamel Sauce to just under boiling and stir in the aspic jelly. Season highly with salt, pepper and cayenne and leave to cool until lukewarm.

8 Using a pastry brush, paint the chilled mousses with the sauce in a series of thin layers. (If the mousses are sufficiently chilled and the layers sufficiently thin, the sauce will set practically on contact.) Coat until the fish is completely masked.

9 Make a final brush-stroke on top of each mousse, and set a basil leaf or sprig of dill into it.

Finnish Herring

[SERVES 4]

1¼ cups thick plain yogurt
¼ cup light cream
1 tbsp. French mustard
1 tbsp. sugar

dill
1 hard-boiled egg, chopped
1 jar (approx 12 oz.) pickled herring

1 Mix everything, except the herring, together very well. Add a little of the liquid from the herring if the mixture is very stiff. Strain the rest of the liquid from the herring and cut the herring into slices. Add the herring to the yogurt mixture and stir to coat well. Refrigerate until required.

M u s s e l   T e r r i n e

[SERVES 6–8]

*The underrated mussel comes into its own in this terrine, at its best made
in late fall or winter, when mussels are in their prime. Use French
bouchots for preference.*

I lb. mussels in their shells
4 tbsp. dry white wine
I tsp. chopped fresh parsley
I tsp. snipped fresh chives
I lb. turbot, chopped
and chilled
salt
lemon juice
2 egg whites
2¼ cups heavy cream, chilled
freshly ground white pepper
I green pepper, diced and
blanched
12 spinach leaves, trimmed
and blanched

¼ lb. shelled cooked shrimp

FOR THE SAUCE
flesh of 4 ripe tomatoes
I tbsp. tarragon vinegar
I½ tbsp. olive oil
I tsp. tomato paste
pinch of sugar
salt and freshly ground
white pepper

FOR THE GARNISH
cilantro or flat-leaf parsley
tomato "roses"

I Discard any mussels that are open. Cook the mussels with the wine
and herbs in a covered, heavy-bottomed pan over a high heat for
about 5 minutes, shaking the pan frequently, until they open. Discard
any that remain closed and remove the others from their shells. Dry
on paper towels.

2 Blend the turbot in a food processor, then mix in the salt and
lemon juice followed by the egg whites. Pass through a strainer into
a bowl placed over a bowl of ice, then gradually work in the cream.
Add white pepper, cover and chill for 30 minutes.

3 Preheat the oven to 300°F. Line the base of a terrine with buttered
parchment paper.

4 Divide the turbot mixture into two thirds and one third. Fold the
green pepper into the larger portion and spread half of this in the
base of the terrine. Cover with half the spinach leaves and lay half the
mussels over them. Fold the shrimp into the remaining turbot
mixture and carefully spread over the mussels. Place the remaining
mussels on top, followed by the remaining spinach leaves. Spread the
remaining green-pepper mixture over the spinach leaves.

5 Cover with buttered parchment paper and stand the terrine in a
roasting or baking pan. Pour in boiling water to surround the terrine
and place in the oven for 1 hour.

6 Purée the tomatoes, vinegar and oil for the sauce, then add the
tomato paste, sugar and seasoning to taste and to adjust the color.
Purée again and chill.

7 Leave the terrine to cool slightly before unmolding.

8 Cut the terrine into slices, place one on each plate and place a
spoonful of the sauce to the side. Garnish with cilantro or flat-leaf
parsley and tomato "roses."

Crab-stuffed Mushrooms

[MAKES 24]

These mushrooms are very rich and very delicious. Even people who usually think they do not like seafood will love this stuffing.

24 large fresh mushrooms
2 tbsp. butter
4 scallions, chopped
I clove garlic, finely chopped
½ tsp. salt
¼ tsp. cayenne

¼ cup dry bread crumbs
¼ cup heavy cream
¾ lb fresh crab meat,
picked over, or frozen or canned,
well drained
freshly grated Parmesan cheese

I Preheat the oven to 350°F. Clean the mushrooms and separate the stems from the caps. Chop the stems finely. Steam the mushrooms for 5 minutes, then set aside.

2 Melt the butter in a skillet over medium heat. Add the chopped stems, scallions and garlic and cook until most of the liquid is evaporated, 8–10 minutes. Add the salt, cayenne, bread crumbs and cream, and mix well. Gently stir in the crab meat and cook until just heated through.

3 Stuff the mushroom caps with the crab mixture, mounding a little on each top. Sprinkle each with Parmesan cheese and arrange on a lightly greased baking sheet. Bake in the oven for 10 minutes, then put under the broiler for 2–3 minutes until the cheese turns golden brown. Serve hot.

Moules à la Marinière

[SERVES 6]

Do not salt this dish at all. And of course, the white wine you swallow with it should be dry as a bone and simple; try a Muscadet from France.

¼ cup butter	I sprig thyme, or ½ tsp. dried thyme
3 shallots, finely chopped	3½ quarts mussels, washed
2 tbsp. chopped fresh parsley	and brushed
I bay leaf	⅔ cup white wine

I Melt the butter in a flameproof casserole with a lid. Soften the shallots in the butter, then add the parsley, bay leaf and thyme. Allow to stew for 30 seconds or so. Discard any mussels that are open.

2 Add the mussels and the white wine and cover. The dish is cooked as soon as steam begins to force its way out of the pot. Serve immediately, or the mussels will toughen. Discard all those still closed.

Seviche of Salmon

[SERVES 4]

The origins of this dish are rooted in the traditional cuisine of South America.

I ¼ lb. skinless salmon fillets, chilled	2 tbsp. green pepper, cut into julienne strips
½ cup lime juice	2 tbsp. chopped shallot
¾ cup lemon juice	salt
½ red chili, seeded	a squeeze of lemon juice
I bunch of fresh cilantro	
3 avocados	FOR THE GARNISH
3 tbsp. crème fraîche	strips of red and green peppers,
2½ tbsp. thyme or	blanched
tarragon vinegar	slices of lemon
I tbsp. Dijon mustard	
2 tbsp. red pepper, cut into julienne strips	

I Cut the salmon into ⅛-in thick slices, about 1-inch square, then lay them in a large, shallow dish.

2 Mix the lime and lemon juice, chili and the stems from the cilantro together and pour over the salmon. Cover and leave in a cool place for 4–5 hours, then drain off the marinade.

3 Purée the flesh from 1 avocado and mix with the marinade, crème fraîche, vinegar, 1½ tbsp. finely chopped cilantro leaves, mustard, peppers, shallot and salt. Pour over the salmon and leave for 10–15 minutes.

4 Peel and slice the remaining avocados. Brush with lemon juice, then arrange in fan shapes on 6 chilled plates. Add the salmon slices.

5 Adjust the seasoning of the dressing if necessary and spoon a little over the salmon. Garnish with strips of red and green peppers and slices of lemon.

Oysters Bienville

Oysters Bienville

[SERVES 3–4]

*Shrimp, mushrooms and Parmesan cheese create a delicious topping that
is a truly wonderful complement to the delicate oyster taste. This dish is
named for Jean Baptiste le Moyne, Sieur de Bienville, founder of
New Orleans.*

Kosher salt
2 tbsp. butter
3 scallions, minced
2 cloves garlic, minced
**1 tbsp. finely chopped
fresh parsley**
**4 large mushrooms,
finely chopped**
1½ tbsp. all-purpose flour
¾ cup heavy cream
**⅓ cup finely chopped cooked
shelled shrimp**
1 egg yolk, lightly beaten

1 tbsp. dry sherry
large pinch of black pepper
large pinch of cayenne
1 tsp. Worcestershire sauce
pinch of salt
16 oysters on the half shell

FOR THE TOPPING
5 tbsp. grated Parmesan cheese
2 tbsp. dry bread crumbs
¼ tsp. salt
large pinch of cayenne
large pinch of black pepper

1 Preheat the oven to 400°F. Pour the Kosher salt about ½ inch deep
into a large roasting pan, or several pans, large enough to hold all the
oysters in one layer, and put in the oven. The salt keeps the oysters
from tipping over, and will help keep them warm after they come out
of the oven.

2 Melt the butter in a skillet over a moderate heat. Sauté the
scallions, garlic, parsley and mushrooms until the vegetables are
limp, about 5 minutes. Add the flour and stir until blended. Add the
cream and stir until blended. Add the shrimp, egg yolk, sherry, black
pepper, cayenne, Worcestershire sauce and salt and cook, stirring,
until the mixture thickens, 5–6 minutes.

3 In a small bowl, make the crumb topping mixture. Combine the
Parmesan cheese, bread crumbs, salt, cayenne and pepper.

4 Put 1 oyster on each half shell and spoon some shrimp sauce over
each oyster. Top each with the crumb mixture. Nestle the oysters in
hot salt. Bake in the oven until the topping is golden, 12–15 minutes.

Deep-fried Oysters

[SERVES 4–6]

*Even people who don't eat oysters will love these hot, crisp finger foods.
Cooked quickly at high heat, the delicate and juicy flavor of the oysters
is sealed in. You may use more cornmeal instead of the cornstarch, and
the result will be a slightly coarser, heavier, but still delicious coating.*

1½ cups cornmeal
4 tbsp. cornstarch
1 tsp. salt
½ tsp. black pepper

½ tsp. cayenne
2 dozen fresh oysters, shelled
vegetable oil for frying

1 Combine all the ingredients, except the oysters and oil. Pat the
oysters dry with paper towels, then dip the oysters in the cornmeal
mixture.

2 In a deep skillet or wok, heat the oil to 365°F. With tongs, drop in
4 or 5 oysters at a time and cook until golden brown, turning once
and making sure they don't touch, about 3 minutes. Drain well on
paper towels and keep warm while you fry the remaining oysters.
Make sure the oil has returned to 365°F before cooking each batch.
Serve hot with Cocktail Sauce (page 51) for dipping the oysters into.

Oysters Rockefeller

[SERVES 4]

An elegant dish for oyster-lovers that combines the mellow tastes of oysters and spinach. This comes from Louisiana where cooks used to flavor it with absinthe, a licorice-flavored liqueur that has been outlawed. Aniseed has been used in this version, but you could also substitute Pernod or any other aniseed-flavored liqueur.

Kosher salt
¼ cup butter
½ lb. fresh spinach, chopped
3 tbsp. chopped fresh parsley
6 scallions, chopped
2 tbsp. finely chopped celery
1 tbsp. finely chopped green pepper
¼ tsp. salt
¼ tsp. aniseed

1½ tsp. fresh thyme, or ½ tsp. dried
1 tbsp. anchovy paste
3 tbsp. dry bread crumbs
½ cup heavy cream
pinch of freshly ground black pepper
few drops of hot-pepper sauce
20 oysters on the half shells

1 Preheat the oven to 400°F. Pour the Kosher salt about ½ inch deep into a large roasting pan, and put into the oven. The salt serves to keep the oysters from tipping over, and it will help keep them warm after they come out of the oven.

2 Melt the butter in a skillet over low heat. Sauté the spinach, parsley, onions, celery and green pepper until the spinach is thoroughly wilted, about 6 minutes. Add remaining ingredients, except the oysters, stirring in a little extra cream or bread crumbs as needed to achieve the consistency of a thick sauce.

3 Put 1 oyster on each half shell and spoon some of the sauce over each oyster. Nestle the oysters in the heated Kosher salt. Bake until the topping is bubbly, about 12 minutes.

Pan-fried Oysters

[SERVES 3–4]

These pan-fried oysters are almost as delicious as deep-fried oysters, but not quite as intimidating for someone who is not adept at deep-frying.

½ cup all-purpose flour	2 eggs, lightly beaten
I cup dry bread crumbs	2 tbsp. milk
½ tsp. salt	2 dozen fresh oysters, shelled
½ tsp. black pepper	½ cup butter
½ tsp. cayenne	lemon wedges, to garnish
¼ tsp. dried thyme	

I Combine the flour, bread crumbs, salt, pepper, cayenne and thyme. In another bowl, combine the eggs and milk.

2 Pat the oysters dry with paper towels. Quickly dip them in the crumb mixture, then in the egg mixture, then again in the crumbs.

3 In a skillet, melt 8 tbsp. butter. Fry some oysters in a single layer until lightly browned on one side, then turn over and cook until the other side is lightly browned. Remove from the skillet and keep warm while you fry the remaining oysters. Add a little more butter to the skillet and fry the next batch. Continue until all the oysters are fried. Serve the oysters with lemon wedges and Cocktail Sauce.

Cocktail Sauce

[MAKES ABOUT I ¼ CUPS]

Prepare this tangy red sauce, with the sharp bite of horseradish, several hours ahead and refrigerate so the flavors blend. Serve with Boiled Shrimp (page 148) or crab, or Deep-fried Oysters (page 49).

½ cup tomato catsup	I tbsp. Worcestershire sauce
½ cup bottled chili sauce	2 scallions, minced
½ tbsp. prepared horseradish	¼ tsp. salt
I tbsp. Dijon-style mustard	¼ tsp. black pepper
I tbsp. freshly squeezed lemon juice	few drops of hot-pepper sauce,
I tbsp. white-wine vinegar	to taste

I In a medium bowl, combine all ingredients and beat together. Refrigerate until ready to serve.

Smoked Herring Pâté

[SERVES 4]

4 frozen smoked herring fillets
I onion, finely chopped
2 tbsp. butter
I tbsp. lemon juice
6 tbsp full-fat cream cheese

I tbsp. sherry
salt and freshly ground
black pepper
fresh parsley sprigs, to garnish

I Place the fish, onion, butter and lemon juice in a microwave-safe dish, cover and cook on Medium for 8–10 minutes, turning and rearranging the fish once.

2 Remove all skin and any bones from the herring fillets, flaking the fish. Purée the flaked herring with the cooking juices and the onion, the cream cheese and sherry in a blender or food processor, then add seasoning to taste.

3 Divide the pâté between 4 individual dishes. Cool and chill well, then garnish with parsley sprigs. Serve with hot toast.

Fish Chowder

[SERVES 4]

I lb. white fish fillet, skinned
2 tbsp. butter
I large onion, finely chopped
I–2 cloves garlic, crushed
4 potatoes, sliced
14-oz. can tomatoes
2–3 fresh thyme sprigs
2–3 fresh parsley sprigs
I–2 bay leaves, or I bouquet garni

salt and freshly ground
black pepper
pinch of cayenne pepper
I ¼ cups boiling water
⅔ cup milk
8 plain crackers, crushed
(optional)
2 tbsp. chopped fresh parsley

I Remove any bones from the fish, then cut into even-sized chunks.

2 Place the butter, onion, garlic and potatoes in a microwave-safe bowl. Cover and cook on Full for 15 minutes, or until the potatoes are almost tender.

3 Add the tomatoes, herbs and seasonings. Pour in the water, then gently stir in the fish.

4 Cover and cook on Full for 8–10 minutes, or until the potatoes are cooked and the fish is firm. Stir halfway through the time to ensure even cooking.

5 Add the milk and heat on Full for 1 minute but do not let the soup boil.

6 Place the crackers in the bottom of individual soup bowls, then ladle the soup on top. Sprinkle with chopped parsley and serve with warm French bread or crispy rolls. Alternatively, omit the crackers and serve the soup straight from the cooking dish.

Mediterranean Fish Soup

[SERVES 4]

¼ cup olive oil
I large onion, finely chopped
2 cloves garlic, crushed
2 celery sticks, sliced
2 × 14-oz cans tomatoes, chopped
⅔ cup dry white wine
2½ cups boiling water
salt and freshly ground black pepper

5 cups mussels, scrubbed and
beards removed
1¼ lb. white fish fillets, skinned
and cut into chunks
I mackerel, skinned, filleted
and cut into chunks
¼ lb. shelled cooked shrimp
chopped fresh parsley, to garnish

I Place the oil, onion and garlic in a microwave-safe bowl and cook on Full for 4 minutes.

2 Add the celery and tomatoes, wine, water and seasoning. Cook on Full for 15 minutes.

3 Discard any opened mussels. Ladle a little of the soup broth into a separate large, microwave-safe bowl and place the washed mussels in it. Cover and cook on Full for 5–8 minutes, stirring once. Discard any unopened mussels, then add the rest to the soup.

4 Place the white fish and mackerel in another microwave-safe dish, cover and cook on Full for 3–4 minutes, or until firm. Add to the soup with the shrimp. Cook on Full for 1–2 minutes to heat before serving, garnished with chopped parsley.

Individual Crab Soufflés

[SERVES 3–6]

2 tbsp. butter
2 tbsp all-purpose flour
salt and freshly ground
black pepper
¼ cup milk
2 egg yolks

4-oz can crab meat,
drained and flaked
I cup grated Gruyère cheese
3 egg whites
a little paprika

I Butter 6 individual microwave-safe soufflé dishes. Place the butter in a large microwave-safe bowl and cook on Full for 1 minute. Stir in the flour and season, then continue to cook for 1–2 minutes.

2 Carefully blend in the milk and cook on Full for 1–2 minutes, stirring once, until the sauce thickens.

3 Stir in the egg yolks, crab meat and cheese; leave to cool.

4 Beat the egg whites until stiff and fold them into the mixture. Divide between the soufflé dishes, dust with paprika and cook on Medium for 7–9 minutes, or until set. Serve at once.

Freshwater fish

Probably the most familiar freshwater fish are salmon and trout, once expensive delicacies to be enjoyed as a treat. With the advent of large-scale fish farming, these are now remarkably good value – and good for health, too. With the new interest in a lowfat diet, fish is high on the shopping list, being a good source of protein without the large quantity of saturated fat that bedevils meat dishes. Now that we cook it more often there is more need to cook it in different ways – and this chapter offers some inspiring dishes to add to your repertoire.

Salmon or Salmon Trout Stuffed with Ripe Olives

[SERVES ABOUT 6]

**1 small salmon or large salmon
trout (about 4½ lb.), cleaned
and scaled
½ lb. fresh or canned
plum tomatoes
¼ cup olive oil
4 cloves garlic, crushed
2 sprigs fresh rosemary**

**6 anchovy fillets
2 tbsp. very finely chopped
ripe olives
2 tbsp. white-wine vinegar
4 tbsp. dry white wine
2 tbsp. brandy
salt and freshly ground black pepper,
to taste**

1 Preheat the oven to 350°F. Roughly chop the tomatoes and spread them out on a large sheet of foil.

2 Mix the olive oil with the chopped tomatoes and lay the fish on top. Smear the inside of the fish with the garlic; lay the sprigs of rosemary and the anchovy fillets at equal intervals inside the cavity. Sprinkle the olives half inside, half outside.

3 Combine the wine vinegar, wine and brandy and pour over the fish. Lift the sides of the foil and seal the fish carefully. Bake for 35 minutes.

4 Lift the fish from the foil with a long metal spatula or pancake turner when it is cooked. Take care when transferring it so that it does not break, and set it on a serving dish.

5 Pour all the juices from the foil into a pan and bring them to a rapid boil. Season with the salt and pepper, pour over the fish and serve.

Salmon en Papillote

[SERVES 2]

Halibut, haddock, trout and indeed almost any fish can be cooked in this way. Papillotes are generally made from circular papers but are better made from heart-shaped pieces if whole small fish or long fillets of fish are to be wrapped.

¼ cup butter	salt and freshly ground
I tbsp. very finely shredded white of leek	black pepper
I tbsp. very finely shredded carrot	10oz fillet of salmon, skinned
⅔ cup very white button mushrooms	2 tbsp. white wine
I tsp. chopped fresh tarragon or fennel leaves	lemon juice
	oil for brushing baking sheet and paper

1 Preheat the oven to 500°F. Cut out 2 "papillotes" of parchment paper circles, 16 inches in diameter.

2 Melt half the butter and add the leek and carrot to it. Cook slowly without browning for 2 minutes, then add the mushrooms. Cook 1 more minute, then add the tarragon or fennel and season with salt and pepper.

3 Cut the salmon fillet into 2 pieces of even thickness.

4 Brush the inside of the paper circles with oil. Lay 1 fish slice on each papillote and cover with the vegetables. Sprinkle each with 1 tbsp. of wine and a few drops of lemon juice. Dot with the remaining butter and add salt and pepper.

5 Fold the free half of the papillote paper over to make a package rather like an apple turnover, and twist to make an airtight seal.

6 Lightly brush a baking sheet with oil and put it into the oven for 5 minutes to heat. Then carefully put the papillotes on the baking sheet, taking care that they do not touch each other. Bake for 5 minutes.

7 Serve immediately on hot, flat plates. The diners unwrap their own puffed-up package, or the cook may serve it for them.

Garlic Gravad Lax

[SERVES 6–8]

A soured cream, mustard and horseradish dressing with a little fresh dill added is excellent with this dish.

2 lb. middle-cut salmon	6 tbsp. sugar
4 cloves garlic, crushed	a handful of chopped fresh dill
6 tbsp. salt	

1 Split the salmon into 2 halves and remove the bone, but leave the skin on. Mix together the remaining ingredients.

2 Place one half of the salmon, skin side down, on a large, flat serving dish and cover with half the mixture. Put the other half of the salmon over it and top with the remaining mixture.

3 Weight down the salmon with a plate and leave in a cool place for at least 24 hours. Scrape off the mixture and serve the salmon cut into thin slices.
Picture on page 54.

Salmon in Pastry with Tarragon Sauce

[SERVES 8–10]

Salmon is expensive. For a cheaper version of this dish use farmed pink trout or any firm-fleshed fish, such as haddock or turbot.

I salmon, about 5 lb. in weight	salt
I lb. store-bought puff pastry dough, thawed if frozen	bones, skin and head from the salmon
a few tbsp. fine semolina	2½ cups water
lemon juice	
about 20 tarragon leaves	**FOR THE SAUCE**
salt and white pepper	½ cup butter, chilled
butter	I tbsp. flour
beaten egg	¼ cup fish stock
	¼ cup white wine
FOR THE STOCK	I tbsp. chopped fresh tarragon or parsley
2 slices onion	2 tbsp. heavy cream
I bay leaf	salt and white pepper
small bunch of parsley	
6 peppercorns	

I Fillet the fish, keeping the fillets intact. Skin the fillets. Use the bones and other trimmings for the stock; put all the stock ingredients into a saucepan and simmer for 30 minutes. Strain into a measuring jug. Make up to 1¼ cups with water if necessary, or boil down to reduce if there is too much liquid.

2 Preheat the oven to 450°F. Roll out one-third of the pastry dough into a long thin piece, about the thickness of a coin. Cut out a fish shape. Place on a wet baking sheet and prick all over. Leave in a cool place for 15 minutes. Bake it in the hot oven until brown and crisp. Cool. Follow the illustrations for the rest of the sequence.

3 Bake for 15 minutes in the hot oven to brown and puff up the pastry, then turn down the oven to 300°F for a further 30 minutes to cook the fish. Cover the crust with wet parchment paper if the pastry looks in danger of over-browning. To test if the fish is cooked, push a skewer through the pastry and fish from the side; it should glide in easily.

4 To make the sauce, melt 2 tbsp. of the butter in a saucepan. Add the flour and cook, stirring, for 1 minute or until the butter and flour are pale biscuit colored and foaming. Remove the saucepan from the heat then add the stock and the wine. Return to the heat and stir until boiling and smooth. Boil rapidly until you have a sauce of coating consistency.

5 Cut the rest of the chilled butter into ½-inch dice. Beat them into the boiling sauce one by one, waiting for each to be incorporated before adding the next. The sauce will thicken perceptibly during this process.

6 Add the chopped fresh tarragon and the heavy cream to the sauce. Season with salt and white pepper as necessary, then pour into a warmed sauceboat.

7 To serve, slide the salmon in pastry onto a board or salmon dish. Hand the sauce separately or slit the salmon down the middle, lift one side of the pastry case, and pour the sauce inside.

Griddled Salmon Steaks
with Herb Butter

Salmon steaks make a quick and delicious meal served with minted new potatoes and green beans.

4 fresh salmon steaks (about 6 oz. each)	I tbsp. chopped fresh parsley
4 oz. butter, softened	I tbsp. chopped fresh tarragon and chives

I Lightly oil a griddle or a heavy pan. Place a salmon steak on the hot griddle and cook for about 4 minutes on each side.

2 Work the butter, the parsley and the tarragon and chives together until you have a herb butter. Serve the steaks on hot plates with knobs of butter on top.

Note: *When fresh herbs are in season, it is a good idea to have a session of making different varieties of herb butter. Herb and garlic butters may be kept in a roll shape in foil and frozen until needed. Soften butter and work in the chopped herbs. Dill, parsley, lemon and tarragon butters are good with fish.*

1 *Cut a fish shape (with a fairly wide tail) out of one-third of the pastry dough, roughly the size of the original fish.*

6 *Using your fingers and a metal spatula, gently lift the base and tuck the margin under it. Brush all over with egg.*

2 *Prick the dough all over to restrict rising and to make it rise evenly. Bake until crisp. If it is soggy underneath, return it to the oven, upside down, for a few minutes.*

4 *Cover the pastry base with the salmon and add lemon juice, tarragon leaves, salt and pepper, and plenty of butter. Take care not to leave the tail section empty.*

7 *To decorate, use a teaspoon to mark fish scales on the body. Use bits of the leftover dough to make a line for the "gills" and give the fish an eye.*

3 *Once baked, sprinkle it heavily with semolina which will prevent the fish juices making the pastry soggy.*

5 *Cover the fish with the remaining dough, rolled to a large sheet. Cut round it, leaving a good 1-inch margin.*

8 *Finally, decorate the tail with strips of dough and brush again with egg.*

Salmon and Vegetable Stir-fry

[SERVES 4]

*Concerning cholesterol, salmon comes into the "medium" category. It is
a rich source of protein, as well as vitamins A and D, and contains two
fatty acids similar to those in polyunsaturated vegetable oils. In this
recipe, a minimal amount of fish is combined with a contrasting mixture
of fresh vegetables.*

6 tbsp sunflower oil
⅔ cup carrots, scraped and cut
into matchstick strips
2 celery sticks, thinly sliced
diagonally
⅔ cup thinly sliced
broccoli spears
4 scallions, trimmed and cut
diagonally into ½-inch pieces
2 tbsp. fresh ginger root, peeled
and finely chopped
2 cloves garlic, finely chopped

6-oz. jar baby corn-on-the-cobs,
drained
2 lb. tail-end salmon, skinned,
boned and cut into thick strips

FOR THE SAUCE
I tbsp. cornstarch
2 tbsp. soy sauce
3 tbsp. sweet sherry
2 tbsp. clear honey
juice of I lemon
2 tbsp. water

I First make the sauce. Put the cornstarch into a small bowl and stir
in the soy sauce. Gradually stir in the remaining ingredients, then set
aside.

2 Heat the oil in a large, shallow skillet or a wok. When it is hot, add
the carrots and celery and stir-fry for 2 minutes. Add the broccoli,
onions, ginger and garlic and continue to stir-fry for 1 minute, then
stir in the baby corn-on-the-cobs.

3 Pour the sauce onto the vegetables and stir for about 1 minute,
until it thickens slightly.

4 Push the vegetables to the sides of the pan and add the salmon in
the center. Stir-fry for 3–4 minutes, until the fish strips turn pale pink.
Serve at once, with brown rice or noodles.

Slices of Salmon with Dill

[SERVES 6]

I lb. salmon fillet, chilled
3 tbsp. lemon juice
salt and freshly ground
white pepper
3 tbsp. butter
2 shallots, finely chopped
¾ cup fish stock
I tbsp. finely chopped celery leaves
3 parsley stems, chopped

4 tbsp. finely chopped dill
I cup full-bodied dry white wine
2 egg yolks
¼ cup heavy cream

FOR THE GARNISH
diamond shapes of red and
green pepper
julienne of lemon peel

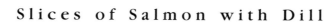

I At least 8 hours before serving, slice the salmon very thinly and lay
the slices in a large, shallow glass dish. Sprinkle with lemon juice and
seasoning, cover and leave in a cool place.

2 Melt the butter and add the shallots. Cover and cook over a
moderate heat, shaking the pan occasionally, until the shallots are
soft. Stir in the stock and reduce to a syrupy glaze. Stir in the celery
leaves, parsley stems, 3 tbsp. dill and the wine. Cover and simmer for

15 minutes. Reduce to ¾ cup. Pass through a strainer. Leave to cool,
then remove the fat from the surface.

3 Just before serving, dry the salmon slices on paper towels. Place 6
plates in a very low oven to warm.

4 Bring the reduced liquid to a boil. Blend the egg yolks and cream
together. Stir in a little of the hot liquid, then stir this mixture into the
remaining liquid and cook over a very low heat, stirring constantly,
until the sauce coats the back of a spoon. Remove from the heat,
season and stir in the remaining dill.

5 Spoon most of the sauce over the plates. Place the salmon slices on
top and trickle the remaining sauce over it. Garnish with the red and
green pepper diamonds and lemon julienne.

Salmon and Vegetable Stir-Fry

Salmon Trout with Champagne Sauce

I salmon trout, approximately 2¼ lb., with head, cleaned	5 green peppercorns
1¾ cups champagne or good-quality sparkling dry white wine	sea salt
I cup fish stock (see page 18)	1¼ cups heavy cream
I sprig fresh tarragon	
I sprig fresh dill	FOR THE GARNISH
	salmon eggs
	sprigs of dill

1 Preheat the oven to 375°F.

2 Place the fish in a fish kettle or a large flameproof casserole. Pour the champagne or sparkling wine and fish stock over and add the herbs, peppercorns and sea salt. Cover closely with buttered parchment paper, then bring just to a boil over a low heat. Transfer to the oven and cook for 20 minutes or until the flesh flakes easily. Carefully transfer the fish to a warmed plate, cover and keep warm.

3 Boil the champagne liquid until reduced by about three-quarters. Strain the liquid and reheat, stirring in the cream. Simmer until thick enough to coat the back of a spoon. Season.

4 Carefully remove the fillets from the fish, discard the skin and place on 4 warmed plates. Spoon a very little of the sauce over the fish and spoon the rest around it. Scatter the salmon eggs over the fish and lay the sprigs of dill on the sauce.

Strips of Salmon with Mushrooms and Quails' Eggs

The superior flavor and texture of wild salmon give the best results in this recipe.

¼ cup butter, diced	FOR THE SAUCE
1¼ lb. wild salmon, cut into strips	1½ cups fruity red wine
salt and freshly ground white pepper	3 tbsp. chopped shallots
½ lb. wild mushrooms	I sprig fresh thyme
4 quails' eggs	I bay leaf
2 tbsp. finely chopped fresh chervil, tarragon, chives and parsley, mixed	I tbsp. fish glaze (see page 18)
	2 tbsp. heavy cream
	¾ cup butter, diced

1 For the sauce, simmer the wine, shallots, thyme and bay leaf until syrupy, then stir in the fish glaze and cream. Pass through a strainer, return to the rinsed-out pan and reheat gently over a very low heat. Gradually stir in the butter, making sure that each piece is fully incorporated before adding the next. Season and keep warm but do not let boil.

2 Heat 1½ tbsp. butter in a skillet. Season the salmon lightly and add to the pan for 2–3 minutes, turning the strips so they cook evenly. Remove with a slotted spoon and drain on paper towels.

3 Add the remaining butter to the pan, then add the mushrooms and cook for 2–3 minutes, depending on the type. Remove with a slotted spoon and drain on paper towels. Sprinkle with seasoning.

4 Meanwhile, cook the quails' eggs in gently boiling water for 2 minutes. Peel, then cut into quarters.

5 Arrange the salmon and mushrooms on 4 warmed plates. Pour the sauce over and arrange the eggs. Sprinkle with the herbs.

Salmon and Spinach Pot Pie

[SERVES 4]

I lb. frozen chopped spinach, cooked
¾ lb. poached, boned and skinned salmon
2½ cups Béchamel Sauce (see page 18)
2 hard-boiled eggs, chopped

I tsp. chopped fresh dill
I tbsp. chopped fresh parsley
salt and freshly ground black pepper
¼ lb. store-bought puff pastry dough, thawed if frozen
½ beaten egg for glazing

I Preheat the oven to 425°F. Cook the frozen spinach in a little salted water as directed on the package. (If using fresh spinach you will need to cook approximately 2 lb.) Drain well and line the bottom of a buttered deep, oval baking dish.

2 Mix the salmon with the Béchamel Sauce (which can be made with fish liquid) and hard-boiled eggs. Mix in the dill and parsley and pour the mixture on top of the spinach.

3 Roll out the puff pastry dough 2 inches larger than the dish. Cut a 1-inch wide strip from the outer edge of the dough. Brush the rim of the dish with water and fit the dough strip around. Lift the remaining piece of dough over the rolling pin and transfer to the dish. Press the edges together and trim with a sharp knife held at an angle away from the dish. To seal the edges firmly together, hold the knife horizontally toward the dish and make a series of shallow cuts around the edge. Flute the edges with thumb and forefinger and pull in the flutes with the back of a knife.

4 To make decorative leaves for a savory pie, cut the remaining dough into 1½-inch strips, using the rolling pin or ruler as a guide. Every 2 inches, cut the strips at an angle to make diamond shapes. Press lines on the diamonds to make the veins of the leaves.

5 Make a hole in the middle of the pie by making a cross with a knife and folding back each part. Arrange the leaves in a decorative pattern around the middle and brush with beaten egg.

6 Bake until the pastry is well risen and golden brown – approximately 30 minutes. Cover with foil if the pastry shows any sign of browning too much.

Salmon Cutlets with Anchovy Butter

[SERVES 4]

4 salmon cutlets
¼ cup anchovy butter
(see page 29)

FOR THE GARNISH
parsley sprigs
4 lemon wedges

I Preheat the broiler to a high heat.

2 Oil the broiler rack. Place each cutlet on the rack to ensure an even heat.

3 Place a small knob of Anchovy Butter (divide a quarter of the mixture in 4) on each cutlet. Broil for 4 minutes.

4 Turn the cutlets with a pancake turner and divide another quarter of the butter among them. Broil on the second side for 4 minutes.

5 Reduce the heat and leave to cook for a further 3 minutes, less if the cutlets are thin.

6 Serve with a neatly arranged pat of Anchovy Butter on top of each cutlet. Garnish with parsley sprigs and lemon wedges.

Coulibac

[SERVES 4]

¼ cup butter
I lb. salmon or salmon trout
salt and freshly ground pepper
8 scallions, washed and chopped,
or I onion, finely chopped
I cup cooked rice
I ½ cups washed and sliced
mushrooms
2 hard-boiled eggs, chopped
grated peel and juice of ½ lemon
I tbsp. chopped fresh dill,
or I tsp. dried

I tbsp. chopped fresh parsley
2 tbsp. sour cream
I lb. store-bought puff pastry
dough, thawed if frozen
I egg, beaten

FOR THE GARNISH
watercress
baked mushrooms

I Preheat the oven to 300°F.

2 Cut half the butter into small pieces and dab over the salmon. Season the salmon and wrap loosely in foil. Place in the oven for 25–30 minutes. Unwrap and allow to cool.

3 Melt the remaining butter. Add the scallions or very finely chopped onion. Gradually stir in the cooked rice and mushrooms. Leave to cool.

4 Remove the skin and bones carefully from the salmon and separate the flesh into large flakes.

5 Mix the salmon in a bowl with the cooked rice and mushrooms, hard-boiled eggs, lemon peel and juice, dill, parsley and seasoning. Lastly add the sour cream.

6 Turn the oven up to 450°F. Roll the dough into 2 squares 14 × 14 inches. Cut into 7-inch squares. Place the mixture in the middle of each square. Dampen the corners, fold the dough over and crimp the edges. Brush with beaten egg and place on a baking sheet in a hot oven for about 20 minutes.

7 Serve garnished with watercress and baked mushrooms and accompanied by Hollandaise Sauce (see page 18) or sour cream mixed with snipped fresh chives.

Salmon Cutlets with Anchovy Butter

Salmon Loaf

[SERVES 8]

5 cups all-purpose flour
I cup unsalted butter, softened
¼ cup margarine
2 tsp. salt
I cup iced water
2 lb. fresh salmon,
skinned and boned
10 cups shredded cabbage
I cup roughly chopped onion

I tsp. black pepper
¾ cup white wine
I lb. mushrooms, quartered
2 egg yolks
I cup chicken stock
4 tbsp. lemon juice
4 tbsp. chopped fresh dill
2 tbsp. sugar
4 hard-boiled eggs, chopped

1 In a large mixing bowl, combine the flour, ¾ cup butter, margarine and 1 tsp. salt. Mix together with a wooden spoon until the dough has a flaky texture. Add the iced water and mix until smooth. Divide the dough into 2 equal portions. Wrap each half in plastic wrap and refrigerate for 3½ hours.

2 Put the salmon, remaining butter, cabbage, onion, pepper, wine, mushrooms, remaining salt, egg yolks, chicken stock, lemon juice, dill and sugar into a large saucepan. Simmer for 1 hour, or until most of the liquid has evaporated.

3 Flake the salmon with a fork. Stir gently and add the chopped hard-boiled eggs. Stir gently again. Set the mixture aside.

4 Roll out half the chilled dough on a lightly floured surface into a rectangle about 1 inch thick. Dust with flour, and then roll the dough out into a sheet ⅛ inch thick. Trim the sheet into a rectangle 8 × 16 inches. Repeat with the remaining dough, but trim the sheet to 10 × 16 inches.

5 Place the smaller dough rectangle on a large, greased baking sheet. Arrange the salmon filling evenly over the dough sheet, leaving a 1-inch border around the edges. Place the larger dough sheet over the filling. Press the edges of the top and bottom dough sheets together with a fork. Chill for 15 minutes.

6 Preheat the oven to 400°F. Bake the loaf for 1 hour. Serve immediately.

Trout al Carpione

[SERVES 6]

6 medium rainbow trout, or
I salmon trout (about 3¼ lb.)
I egg
1¼ cups olive oil
I cup all-purpose flour
I large onion, very finely sliced
4 cloves garlic

⅔ cup dry white wine
2 tbsp. vinegar
2 tbsp. sugar
2 large sprigs fresh rosemary
4 fresh bay leaves
I chili pepper
salt to taste

1 Clean and dry the fish. If you are using salmon trout, cut it into slices about ½-inch thick.

2 Beat the egg and mix with its own volume of water.

3 Heat about one-third of the oil to a medium heat. Dip the whole fish or slices in the egg/water mixture and then roll in the flour. Fry gently until cooked – the whole trout 8 minutes per side, the slices 4–5. When cooking fish in this way *turn it once only*.

4 Carefully remove the fish when it is cooked and arrange it on a serving dish.

5 Set the rest of the olive oil on a medium heat and sweat the onion in the oil. Add the garlic and cook both together until the onion is completely soft. Neither must brown.

6 Add the wine, vinegar, sugar, rosemary, bay leaves and the whole chili. Bring everything to a boil and season. Pour the mixture over the fish and serve – warm, cool or chilled.

Trout Chaudfroid

[SERVES 4]

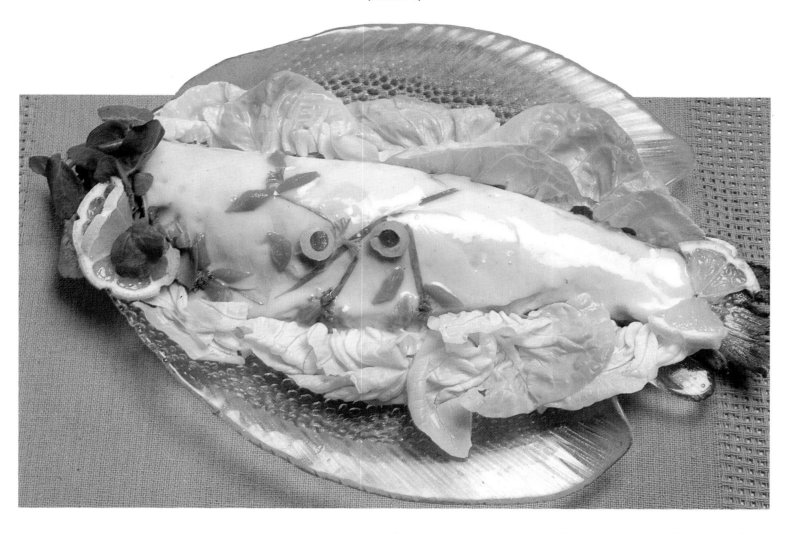

4 trout
1¼ cups Chaudfroid Sauce
(see page 20)

FOR THE GARNISH
cucumber peel
canned pimiento
stuffed olives, sliced
watercress

1 Cook the trout "au bleu" (see page 73) and leave to cool.

2 Remove the heads and top skin. Lift the top fillet carefully from the fish and remove the bone. Lay the fillet back on the fish.

3 Coat the fish with sauce. Garnish with cucumber peel cut into thin strips, diamond-shaped pieces of pimiento and sliced stuffed olives to make flowers and leaves. Surround the head end with sprigs of watercress.

Trout with Cucumber Sauce

[SERVES 4]

This light main-course fish dish, which needs no other accompaniment except wine, is an ideal choice for a summer luncheon.

3 tbsp. butter, chopped	6 tbsp. good-quality sparkling
I shallot, finely chopped	dry white wine
4 trout, filleted and skinned	½ cup heavy double cream
salt and freshly ground	
white pepper	FOR THE GARNISH
½ cup dry white vermouth	baby new potatoes
I ¼ cups fish stock	small balls of pea purée or pea and
½ large, firm cucumber, peeled,	mint purée
seeded and chopped	concassé tomatoes
I sprig fresh thyme	

I Melt 1 tbsp. butter in a skillet. Add the shallot and cook gently for 2–3 minutes.

2 Cut each trout fillet into 3 strips lengthwise. Lay them on top of the shallot. Season them and pour the vermouth over them. Cover with buttered parchment paper and cook over a low heat for about 2 minutes until the flesh is just opaque. Transfer to a warmed dish, cover and keep warm.

3 Add the stock, cucumber and thyme and reduce by three-quarters. Remove the thyme. Purée the sauce, then pass through a strainer. Add the sparkling wine and cream and simmer for about 3 minutes. Gradually swirl in the remaining butter over a low heat.

4 Meanwhile, cook the baby new potatoes in a steamer and warm the balls of purée on a piece of foil on top of it.

5 Coat 4 warmed plates with the sauce. Arrange the strips of trout on the sauce and arrange the potatoes and purée around. Finish with the tomato.

Trout with Almond-Yogurt Sauce

[SERVES 4]

You could, of course, use this sauce with other fish, but the traditional combination of trout with almonds works particularly well.

4 trout, cleaned	½ cup blanched almonds,
I ¼ cups fish stock	finely ground
I ½ tbsp. cornstarch	salt and pepper
2 tbsp. water	⅓ cup flaked almonds, toasted
⅔ cup plain yogurt	

I Either broil or bake the trout. While they are cooking, prepare the sauce. Heat the stock. Mix the cornstarch and water to a smooth paste and stir it into the yogurt. Add the yogurt mixture to the stock, together with the ground almonds and salt and pepper. Cook on a low heat for 5 minutes and then keep warm until the trout are ready.

2 Place the fish on a heated serving dish and scatter over the toasted almonds. Serve the sauce separately.

Poached Trout

[SERVES 4]

A simple method for serving delicate, pink-fleshed trout.

2 ½ cups water	4 trout, cleaned with heads on
I small onion, sliced	¼ cup butter
I bay leaf	
I sprig fresh parsley	FOR THE GARNISH
salt and freshly ground	2 eggs, hard-boiled and chopped
black pepper	I tbsp chopped fresh dill

I Pour the water into a large, shallow pan and add the onion, bay leaf, parsley and seasoning. Heat gently until simmering, then cook for 5 minutes.

2 Reduce the heat so that the liquid barely simmers and add the trout. Cook very gently for 5–7 minutes, turning the trout over once, until cooked through. Meanwhile, melt the butter in a small saucepan.

3 Transfer the trout to a warmed serving platter. Carefully remove the skin, using the point of a knife. Turn each fish over and remove the skin from the second side. Pour the hot butter over and garnish with chopped egg. Sprinkle with dill and serve at once.

Smoked Eel Salad

[SERVES 4]

*Smoked eel makes a tasty salad which may be served with vegetables or
with thinly sliced rye bread.*

½ lb. smoked eel fillet
4 small tomatoes, thinly sliced
2 tbsp. finely chopped onion
1 tbsp. vinegar
1 tsp. sugar
2 tsp. water

1 small lettuce heart, shredded
salt and freshly ground
black pepper
¼ cup soured cream
a little paprika

1 Cut each piece of eel in half lengthwise and pick out all the bones. Arrange the strips of eel on individual plates with the tomato slices. Sprinkle the onion over the tomato.

2 Stir the vinegar, sugar and water together until the sugar has dissolved. Toss this dressing with the lettuce and seasoning to taste. Arrange the lettuce on the plates. Top the fillets of eel with a little soured cream and sprinkle with paprika.

Salmon Steaks with Hollandaise Sauce

[SERVES 2]

The salmon steaks can be served cold but they should not be chilled before serving. If cooling the fish, make the sauce just before it is to be served. New potatoes and young peas make a good accompaniment.

½ cup butter, diced
2 tbsp. lemon juice
3 egg yolks

salt and freshly ground white pepper
4 salmon steaks
(about 6 oz. each)

1 Put the butter in a microwave-safe bowl and cook on Medium for 2 minutes, or until melted. Add the lemon juice and the egg yolks and beat lightly.

2 Cook on Medium for 1 minute, beat again and season to taste. Transfer the sauce to a heated sauce boat and keep warm while you cook the salmon.

3 Place the fish steaks in a shallow microwave-safe dish. Cover and cook on Full for 3½–4 minutes, rearranging the steaks and turning them over once during cooking. Serve with the sauce poured over.

Trout Stuffed with Watercress

[SERVES 4]

I tbsp. butter
I clove garlic, crushed
I bunch watercress, trimmed
and chopped
4 tbsp. bread crumbs

I egg, beaten
4 small trout
salt and freshly ground
black pepper

1 First make the stuffing. Put the butter in a microwave-safe bowl and cook on Full for 30 seconds. Add the garlic and cook on Full for 1 minute.

2 Mix together the watercress, bread crumbs, garlic butter and beaten egg. Season to taste and stuff the trout with this mixture.

3 Lay the trout in a microwave-safe dish and cover with vented plastic wrap. Cook on Full for 4 minutes, rearranging once, until done.

4 Serve with mashed potatoes and a tomato salad.

Trout with Cucumber and Mushroom

[SERVES 4]

¼ cucumber, sliced
1⅓ cups sliced mushrooms
⅔ cup canned consommé
4 small trout of even size
4 tbsp. water

FOR THE GARNISH
parsley
lemon wedges

1 Put the cucumber and mushrooms in a microwave-safe dish and pour the consommé over them. Cover with vented plastic wrap and cook on Full for 4 minutes. Set aside.

2 Put the trout in a microwave-safe dish. Add the water, cover with vented plastic wrap and cook on Full for 4 minutes, turning once, until cooked through.

3 Put the trout on heated plates and pour the sauce over.

4 Serve garnished with parsley and lemon wedges.

Eels with Peas and Parsley Sauce

[SERVES 4]

1½ lb. eel, skinned, boned and
cut into 2-inch pieces
⅔ cup fish stock, boiling
(or see method)
2 slivers of lemon
3 tbsp. butter

4 tbsp. all-purpose flour
⅔ cup milk
salt and freshly ground
black pepper
2 tbsp. chopped fresh parsley
7-oz. can peas, drained

1 Put the eels in a deep, oblong microwave-safe dish and add the boiling fish stock. Alternatively, use the liquid from the canned peas. Add the lemon slivers, cover with vented plastic wrap and cook on Full for 5 minutes, until tender. Discard the lemon.

2 Put the butter in a microwave-safe measuring jug and cook on Full for 45 seconds. Stir in the flour. Pour in the milk and the cooking liquid from the eels and cook on Full for 3 minutes, beating after each minute. Season and stir in the parsley.

3 Add the peas to the dish of eels and pour the sauce over. Reheat for 1 minute, then serve with mashed potatoes.

Sea fish

With the efficient refrigeration facilities on modern fishing trawlers, the produce at our fish merchants and supermarkets is fresher and more varied than ever before. We now buy as a matter of course types of fish that were barely heard of a dozen years ago, and cook them in both new and familiar ways. Many of the recipes in this chapter suit any of a range of white fish, while others are designed for the special flavors of fish such as skate and monkfish.

Garlic Mackerel with Sharp Gooseberry Sauce

[SERVES 4]

2 large, fresh mackerel
2 small lemons
3 cloves garlic, peeled
2 tbsp. oil

salt and pepper
¾ lb. sharp, green gooseberries
a little sugar (optional)

1 Wash and gut the mackerel, and cut 3 or 4 diagonal slashes down the side of each fish.

2 Cut 1 of the lemons and 1 of the garlic cloves into 4 slices, and put 2 pieces of each inside each fish.

3 Juice the remaining lemon, crush the rest of the garlic and combine with the oil, a little salt and plenty of black pepper. Pour over the fish. Leave the mackerel to marinate in a cool place for 2–4 hours.

4 To make the sauce, top and tail the gooseberries, then cook in a covered pan with a little water over a low heat until tender. Add sugar to taste and strain the fruit.

5 To cook the mackerel, drain off the marinade. Broil under a moderate heat for 20–25 minutes, turning once and basting from time to time with the marinade. Serve with the warm sauce and sweet potatoes.

Goujons of Brill
with Red Currant Dressing

4 fillets of brill, each approximately 6 oz., skinned and cut into strips	I ½ tbsp. finely chopped shallot
	½ tbsp. finely snipped chives
	7 oz. red currants
oak leaf lettuce	salt and freshly ground black pepper
FOR THE DRESSING	
3 tbsp. champage vinegar	**FOR THE GARNISH**
4½ fl. oz. olive oil	red currants
3 tbsp. red currant juice	sprigs of chervil

I Shake all the ingredients for the dressing together.

2 Steam the brill for about 5 minutes until just opaque – take care not to overcook. Remove the brill from the heat, cover and keep warm.

3 Gently warm the dressing. Meanwhile, arrange the lettuce on 4 large chilled plates.

4 Arrange the brill in the center of the plates and spoon the dressing over. Garnish with red currants and sprigs of chervil.

Panache of Seafood

[SERVES 4]

Start to cook the seabass and monkfish before adding the John Dory and then the scallops to the steamer, because the more delicate fish will become too tough if cooked for the same length of time as the firmer ones.

¼ lb. skinned, boned salmon	freshly ground white pepper
salt	4 scallops
½ tsp. egg white	¾ lb. John Dory fillets
⅔ cup heavy cream, chilled	½ lb. sea bass fillets
cayenne pepper	½ lb. monkfish fillets
a few strands of saffron	
I cup fish stock	**FOR THE GARNISH**
½ cup dry white wine	sprigs of cilantro and chervil
I ½ tsp. lemon juice	

I Purée the salmon in a food processor or blender. Add the salt and then the egg white. Pass through a strainer into a bowl over a bowl of ice, then gradually beat in the chilled cream. Add a little cayenne pepper, cover and chill for 30 minutes.

2 Pipe the salmon mixture into 4 small decorative molds, pushing it well into the sides. Place the molds in a shallow pan, surround with hot water, place over a low heat and poach for 10 minutes. Leave to stand off the heat for 2 minutes.

3 Stir the saffron into a little of the stock. Bring the remaining stock, wine and lemon juice to a boil and reduce by three-quarters. Stir in the cream and saffron liquid and simmer for 2 minutes. Season and add a little more lemon juice if needed.

4 Open the scallops and cut the other fish into 4 pieces each. Season the fish and steam for 3–5 minutes until just opaque.

5 Unmold the salmon onto 4 plates. Spoon the sauce around and place the fish on top. Garnish with cilantro and chervil.

Roulade of Sole

[SERVES 4]

6 poached crayfish, shelled
3 tbsp. heavy cream
salt and freshly ground
white pepper
4 fillets of sole, skinned
court-bouillon (see page 19)

FOR THE SAUCE
¼ cup fish stock
I cup full-bodied dry white wine
6 tbsp. butter, diced
salt and freshly ground
white pepper

1 Peel the crayfish and remove the veins running down the back. Chop the flesh coarsely, then process briefly in a food processor. Add the cream and seasoning and mix briefly. Pass through a fine strainer.

2 Lightly season the skinned side of the sole then spread the crayfish mixture in a line down the center. Fold the sides of the sole over the filling. Place with the join underneath in the top half of a steamer. Put the lid on.

3 Heat some court-bouillon to simmering point in the bottom half of the steamer. Put the top half in place and cook the fish for about 5 minutes until just opaque.

4 Meanwhile, reduce the fish stock and wine for the white sauce to 4 tbsp. Reduce the heat to very low, then gradually stir in the butter, making sure that each piece is fully incorporated before adding the next. Season and keep warm but do not let boil.

5 Remove the fish from the heat. Trim the ends from the fillets, then cut each into 6 slices and arrange on 4 warmed plates.

Poached Sole

[SERVES 6]

¾ cup dry vermouth
2 large onions, sliced
4 fresh parsley sprigs
I bay leaf
2 tbsp. chopped fresh basil leaves,
or I tsp. dried basil
I tbsp. black pepper
I cup chopped celery

3¾ cups water
½ tsp. dried thyme
salt
4 lb. sole or flounder fillets
6 tomatoes
4 egg yolks, beaten
I cup heavy cream

1 To make the poaching liquid, combine the vermouth, onions, parsley, bay leaf, basil, black pepper, celery, water, thyme and salt in a large pot. Simmer over a low heat for 30 minutes.

2 Arrange the fillets on a large square of cheesecloth. Top with the tomatoes and wrap with the cheesecloth.

3 Strain the broth into a fish poacher or large skillet. Add the wrapped fish and tomatoes. Cover and simmer gently over a low heat for 10 minutes.

4 Remove the fish and tomatoes from the poacher. Remove the cheesecloth and arrange the fillets on a warm serving platter. Keep warm while you make the sauce.

5 Beat the egg yolks and cream into the remaining broth in the poacher. Cook over a medium heat, stirring constantly, for 5 minutes or until the sauce thickens. Do not let boil. Pour the sauce over the fish and serve with lemon slices.

Sole Bonne Femme

[SERVES 6]

3 Dover sole of about
I lb. each, filleted
I small onion, very finely chopped
⅔ cup white wine
⅔ cup fish stock
(see page 18)

3 cups sliced mushrooms
Hollandaise Sauce made with 2
egg yolks and ⅔ cup butter
(see page 18)
salt and pepper to taste

1 Place the sole fillets, onion, white wine and fish stock in a pan and poach over a gentle heat for about 5 minutes.

2 Retrieve the sole fillets from the liquid, set aside, and reduce the pan juices until they are almost a glaze. Add the mushrooms and poach for 2–3 minutes. Add the glazed mushrooms to the Hollandaise Sauce. Season.

3 Arrange the sole fillets on a flameproof dish. Coat with the sauce and glaze for 2–3 minutes under the hottest broiler you can manage. Serve immediately.

Sole with Snow Peas

[SERVES 4]

¼ lb. snow peas
2 small carrots, cut into julienne
salt and freshly ground
white pepper
8 fillets of sole,
cut in half lengthwise
16 very thin slices of fresh ginger
root, cut into strips
8 scallions, cut in half
lengthwise

2 tsp. olive oil
peel of 2 oranges, cut into short
julienne
1 tbsp. very finely chopped
ginger root
2 tbsp. soy sauce
7 tbsp. fino sherry
a squeeze of lemon juice
4 tbsp. water

1 Arrange the snow peas and carrots in a large steamer or 2 small ones. Sprinkle with salt and freshly ground white pepper. Season the skin side of the pieces of sole, then roll them up loosely, seasoned side innermost, starting from the narrow end. Place a little way apart on the vegetables. Place a piece of ginger and a scallion half on each piece of fish.

2 Place the steamer over a pan of simmering water and steam for about 8 minutes until the sole is just opaque all the way through.

3 Meanwhile, heat the oil. Add the orange julienne and cook until just beginning to curl. Stir in the chopped ginger and cook for about 30 seconds, then stir in the soy sauce, sherry, lemon juice and water. Bring to a boil, then reduce the heat and simmer for 5 minutes.

4 Spoon the sauce onto parts of 4 warmed plates. Carefully place the rolls of sole on the sauce. Scatter the orange julienne on the rolls and garnish the plates with the vegetables.

Fried Fillets of Sole with Cucumber

[SERVES 4]

3 large lemon soles
I large cucumber
seasoned flour
6–8 tbsp. butter

salt and pepper
2 tsp. lemon juice
2 tsp. chopped fresh parsley

1 Skin and fillet the soles into 12 neat fillets.

2 Peel the cucumber and, using a melon-baller, scoop the flesh into balls. Place these in a pan of boiling salted water for 2–3 minutes. Drain and dry well.

3 Dip the fillets in seasoned flour. Lay them on a plate but do not let them touch each other – they will become soggy and will not fry well.

4 Heat 1 good tbsp. butter in a skillet. When foaming, put in the fillets – not too many at a time. Turn them over when a golden brown; allow about 1½ minutes on each side. Place in a shallow platter and keep warm. (Halfway through the cooking, if the butter over-browns, it will be necessary to wipe the pan out and then reheat with fresh butter.)

5 Melt more butter in the pan. Add the cucumber balls and fry quite briskly until a delicate brown. Leave the pan to cool for a minute. Add salt, pepper, parsley and lemon juice. Boil up and tip over the fish. Serve immediately.

Smoked Fish Pie

[SERVES 4–6]

2½ cups Béchamel Sauce
(see page 18)
7 tbsp. dry white wine
2 tbsp. light cream
¾ lb. smoked haddock, cooked,
boned and skinned (other
firm-fleshed smoked fish can be
used)

6 oz. cooked shelled shrimp
1½ cups button mushrooms,
cooked
1 tbsp. snipped fresh chives and
chopped parsley
salt and pepper
¾ lb. store-bought puff pastry
dough
milk or egg, to glaze

1 Preheat the oven to 425°F. Pour the Béchamel Sauce into a bowl. Add the wine and cream, then mix in all the other ingredients, except for the salt and pepper, dough and glaze.

2 Season to taste and place in a buttered deep, oval baking dish. Cover with puff pastry dough. Glaze with milk or a beaten egg, and bake for 15–20 minutes.

Soy-Braised Sliced Fish

[SERVES 4–6]

1½ lb. fish steak, such as cod,
haddock, halibut and mullet
1½ tsp. salt
pepper to taste
½ cup vegetable oil
1½ tbsp. cornstarch

3 scallions
4 slices fresh ginger root
3 tbsp. soy sauce
3 tbsp. stock (see page 18)
1½ tbsp. dry sherry
2 tsp. sugar

1 Cut the fish into 2½×1½×1 inch pieces. Toss in the salt, pepper and 2 tsp. of the oil. Dust in the cornstarch. Cut the spring scallions into 1-inch sections, separating the green from the white parts. Combine the soy sauce, stock, sherry and sugar into a sauce.

2 Heat the oil in a wok or skillet. When hot, stir-fry the ginger and white parts of the scallions for about 15 seconds to flavor the oil. Add the fish pieces, one by one, spacing them in the pan. Fry for 1½ minutes on either side. Drain off the excess oil. Pour the sauce over the fish pieces. Sprinkle with the green parts of the scallions and bring to a boil. Baste the fish with the boiling sauce, turning the fish after 1½ minutes. Simmer for another 2 minutes and then transfer to a heated plate. Pour the sauce and scallions over the fish.

Cod Baked with Bacon

[SERVES 4–6]

This dish is also good cooked without the cream, but it must be covered with foil from the beginning of the cooking.

1 Spanish onion, sliced
6 tbsp. butter
1 lb. potatoes, parboiled and
thinly sliced
salt and pepper
4 good-sized cod steaks, or firm
white fish steaks of your choice

½ lb. lean smoked
streaky bacon
1¼ cups heavy cream or milk
chopped fresh parsley

1 Preheat the oven to 350°F. Soften the onion in 4 tbsp. butter and place some of it in the bottom of a baking dish. Put the sliced potato on top and season. Put the cod steaks on top of the potatoes and cover with the rest of the onion and the bacon.

2 Place in the oven. After 15 minutes pour the cream into the dish, dot with the remaining butter and replace in the oven for another 40 minutes. Garnish with parsley and serve with a green salad.

Fish Balls

[SERVES 4]

*These fish Balls may be served as part of a salad, as below, or they may be
served hot, coated with horseradish sauce made in the same way as in
Fish in Horseradish Sauce (right).*

I small onion, finely chopped
2 tbsp. butter
½ cup fresh white bread crumbs
¾ lb. cod fillet, skinned
I egg white
2 tbsp. chopped fresh dill
salt and freshly ground
white pepper
3¾ cups fish stock

white part of I leek, thinly sliced
I lettuce heart, shredded
¼ cucumber, thinly sliced
(about ¼ lb.)
8 radishes, sliced
7 tbsp. mayonnaise
7 tbsp. soured cream
dill sprigs, to garnish

I Cook the onion in the butter for about 10 minutes, until soft but not browned. Mix with the bread crumbs in a bowl. Grind the fish or purée it in a food processor and add it to the crumb mixture. Stir in the egg white, dill and plenty of seasoning.

2 Using wet hands, roll small portions of the fish mixture into walnut-sized balls. The mixture should make 16 balls. Heat the fish stock in a saucepan until simmering. Add the fish balls and simmer for 10 minutes. Drain and cool.

3 Blanch the leek in boiling water for 30–60 seconds, drain immediately and rinse under cold water. Drain and pat dry on paper towels. Arrange the lettuce, leek and cucumber on individual plates or on a large platter. Group the fish balls on the salad, adding the radish slices for color.

4 Mix the mayonnaise and soured cream with a little seasoning to taste. Spoon this dressing over the fish balls. Garnish with dill and serve.

Fish in Horseradish Sauce

[SERVES 4]

This simple dish of cod in a creamy horseradish sauce is quite delicious.

**I lb. cod fillet, skinned and
cut into 4 portions
2 bay leaves
salt and freshly ground
black pepper
I cup water
2 tbsp. butter**

**¼ cup all-purpose flour
3 tbsp. grated horseradish
I ¼ cups soured cream**

**FOR THE GARNISH
dill or parsley sprigs
lemon slices**

I Place the fish in a skillet and add the bay leaves. Sprinkle with seasoning, pour in the water and heat gently until simmering. Cook gently for 3–5 minutes, until the fish is just cooked. Use a pancake turner to transfer the pieces of fish to a baking dish. Strain the fish cooking liquid and reserve.

2 Preheat the oven to 425°F. Melt the butter in a small saucepan and stir in the flour. Gradually pour the reserved fish cooking liquid onto the flour mixture, stirring all the time. Add the horseradish and bring to a boil to make a very thick sauce. Stir in a little seasoning and the soured cream. Spoon the sauce over the fish.

3 Bake for about 10 minutes, until the sauce is just beginning to brown. Garnish with dill and lemon, then serve at once.

Kedgeree

[SERVES 4–6]

Kedgeree is an Anglo-Indian dish which is good for breakfast, lunch or supper.

2 lb. smoked haddock or cod
I bay leaf
3½ cups basmati or
long-grain rice
I cup unsalted butter
I tbsp. curry powder
I¼ cups Béchamel Sauce
(see page 18)

8 hard-boiled eggs, chopped

FOR THE GARNISH
chopped fresh cilantro
lemon slices

1 Cover the fish with cold water and add a bay leaf. Bring to a boil and turn off the heat. Remove the fish and reserve the water.

2 Cook the rice in ½ cup butter and the fish water, adding extra cold water if necessary. There should be double the volume of water to rice. Cook the rice until most of the water has been absorbed and holes appear on the surface. Turn off the heat, cover and leave in a warm place or low oven while you deal with the fish.

3 Remove all bones and skin from the fish. Melt the rest of the butter and add the curry powder. Cook for 2 minutes and add the fish.

4 Make the Béchamel Sauce and add to the fish and butter. Cook for 2 minutes. Then gently fold into the rice, which should now be perfectly cooked, making sure all the grains are equally coated. Then mix in the hard-boiled eggs.

5 Serve in a large warm bowl, garnished with fresh cilantro and lemon slices.

Smoked Haddock Lasagne

[SERVES 6–8]

12 cloves garlic, unpeeled
1 ½ lb. smoked haddock fillets
1 ¼ cups milk
a pinch of saffron threads
(optional)
½ bay leaf
1 medium onion, thinly sliced
¼ cup butter
¼ cup all-purpose flour
1 tbsp. grated Parmesan cheese

3 hard-boiled eggs
salt and pepper
¾ lb. dry green lasagne
a little oil
¾ lb. ripe tomatoes, peeled
and thinly sliced
1 tsp chopped fresh basil
6 oz. mozzarella cheese,
thinly sliced

1 Plunge the unpeeled garlic cloves into boiling water and simmer for 20–25 minutes, until soft. Drain, peel and mash.

2 Poach the fish in the milk with the saffron and the bay leaf for about 10 minutes or until the flesh is firm and flakes easily. Lift the fish carefully out of the milk, skin if necessary, and break into bite-sized pieces with a fork. Discard the bay leaf and any bits of fish left in the milk.

3 Sweat the onion in the butter until transparent, taking care not to let it brown. Stir in the flour and cook for several minutes more.

4 Add the milk, a little at a time and let the sauce simmer for 5 minutes.

5 Remove from the heat and stir in the Parmesan cheese, mashed garlic, fish pieces, and the hard-boiled eggs cut into eighths. Season well with salt and pepper and leave, covered, in a cool place until needed.

6 Preheat the oven to 425°F. Boil the lasagne in batches in lots of salted water with a little oil to stop them sticking together. They should take between 10 and 20 minutes to cook until *al dente*. Lift each piece of cooked pasta out, run under cold water and lay on a damp dishtowel.

7 When all the pieces of lasagne are cooked, use some of them to line the bottom and sides of a well-greased small, deep roasting pan or large baking dish and spread half the fish mixture over them.

8 Top with half the tomatoes, sprinkled with half the basil. Add another layer of pasta, fish, tomatoes and basil, finishing up with a layer of pasta.

9 Spread the sliced mozzarella over the top and bake for approximately 30 minutes, until the top is crisped and well browned.

Baked Smoked Haddock

[SERVES 4]

1 ½ lb. smoked haddock fillets
3 eggs
2 cups plain yogurt

freshly ground black pepper
2 tbsp. grated Parmesan cheese
(optional)

1 Preheat the oven to 350°F. Poach the smoked haddock, drain it very well and flake the flesh. Mix the eggs and yogurt together with some pepper. Stir this through the fish. Put the mixture into a greased shallow baking dish, sprinkle over the grated Parmesan and bake, uncovered, for 20 minutes. Add some cooked rice before baking if you like. or use the mixture as a filling for a quiche.

Fried Fish with Mushroom Sauce

[SERVES 4]

One dried mushroom is sufficient to flavor a tempting sauce that enlivens plainly cooked fish.

4 herrings or small mackerel,
cleaned with heads off
¼ cup all-purpose flour
salt and freshly ground
black pepper
4 tbsp. oil

FOR THE SAUCE
I large dried mushroom

I ¼ cups water
I onion, finely chopped
2 tbsp. butter
2 tbsp. all-purpose flour
⅔ cup soured cream

FOR THE GARNISH
8 thin lemon wedges
4 dill or parsley sprigs

I Bone the fish. Coat in the flour and plenty of seasoning, then set aside.

2 For the sauce, simmer the mushroom in the water, covered, for 5 minutes. Lift the mushroom from the liquid and chop finely. Gently cook the onion in the butter in a small saucepan for about 10 minutes until well cooked but not browned. Stir in the flour, then gradually add the mushroom liquid, stirring all the time. Bring the sauce to a boil and add the chopped mushroom. Season the sauce, simmer for 1 minute, then stir in the soured cream. Keep the sauce warm but do not let boil.

3 Heat the oil in a skillet and cook the fish until well browned on both sides. Drain on paper towels before transferring to a warmed serving platter or 4 plates. Pour a little of the sauce over the fish and serve the rest separately. Garnish with lemon and dill, then serve immediately.

Baked Fish with Sour Cream

1 ½ lb. fish fillets (haddock,
cod, halibut, lemon sole)
I large onion, thinly sliced
2 tsp. cornstarch
2 tbsp. water

I cup sour cream
¼ cup butter, melted
2 tsp. paprika
salt and pepper

I Preheat the oven to 350°F. Place the fish in a shallow baking dish and cover with the sliced onion. Mix the cornstarch with the water to a smooth paste and stir this into the sour cream. Spoon it over the fish. Drizzle the melted butter on top. Sprinkle over the paprika and salt and pepper. Bake, covered, for 45 minutes.

Fish in Deviled Cream

[SERVES 4]

4 firm, white fish steaks
2 tbsp. butter
⅔ cup chilled cream,
whipping or heavy

Itsp English mustard
I tbsp. Worcestershire sauce
salt and hot-pepper sauce, to taste
I tbsp. chutney (optional)

I Preheat the oven to 350°F. Arrange the fish steaks in a greased baking dish, dot with butter, cover the whole dish with foil and bake until the fish is just firm and flakes easily, about 25 minutes.

2 Whip the cream. Lightly stir into it the mustard and Worcestershire sauce and season with a little salt and plenty of hot-pepper sauce. Finally fold in the chutney, if used.

3 Mask the cooked fish steaks with the deviled cream and increase the heat to 425°F; bake for 7–10 minutes. Serve immediately.

Soused Herrings with Sour Cream

[SERVES 2–4]

6 fresh herring fillets
· I large Spanish onion,
thinly sliced
6 bay leaves
18 whole black peppercorns

1¼ cups red-wine vinegar
mixed with water
1¼ cups sour cream
fresh dill, chopped

1 Preheat the oven to 325°F. Wash the herring fillets and pat them dry with paper towels.

2 Place some of the onion, a bay leaf, and three whole peppercorns on each fish. Roll up the herrings with the tail-end away from you.

Place in a baking dish and cover with the vinegar and water mixture.

3 Place in the oven until the herrings are cooked – about 20 minutes. Let the fish cool in the liquid for several hours or overnight.

4 Serve cold with a spoonful of sour cream garnished with chopped dill.

Herring and Bean Salad

[SERVES 4]

I cup dried butter beans
soaked overnight in cold water
to cover
salt and freshly ground
black pepper
4 salted herring fillets
2 tbsp. olive oil
I medium potato,
cooked and diced

I pickled cucumber, sliced
⅓ cup cooked peas
4 tbsp. soured cream
4 tbsp. mayonnaise
2 tbsp. chopped fresh dill or
parsley
2 tbsp. finely chopped onion
I tsp. grated lemon peel
lemon wedges, to garnish

1 Drain the soaked beans. Cook them in plenty of fresh, boiling water for 1 hour, until tender. Add salt to the water halfway through cooking. Drain well and cool.

2 Cut the herring fillets into strips and mix with the cooled beans and olive oil. Add the potato, pickled cucumber and peas, mixing lightly to avoid breaking up the ingredients. Transfer to individual bowls or a large dish.

3 Mix the soured cream, mayonnaise, dill, onion, lemon peel and seasoning to taste. Spoon this dressing over the salad and add lemon wedges to garnish. The dressing should be tossed into the ingredients just before the salad is eaten. Lemon juice may be squeezed over to sharpen the salad.

Flounder with Mustard Sauce

[SERVES 4]

4 flounder fillets
2 shallots, chopped
2 tbsp. Dijon mustard

I ¼ cups light cream
watercress

1 Preheat the oven to 350°F. Butter an enamel or glass baking dish. Place the fish fillets in the dish.

2 Mix the shallots, mustard and cream together. Pour over the flounder and bake in a moderate oven for 15–20 minutes.

3 Serve with bunches of watercress.

Marinated Fish

[SERVES 4]

Use the freshest possible fish. If you are using mackerel look for small, young specimens that tend to be fine-flaked and not overrich. The fish rolls may be served with boiled potatoes and beet salad, or accompanied by rye bread.

**2½ cups water
I bay leaf
I onion, thinly sliced
salt and freshly ground
black pepper
2 tbsp. vinegar
4 mackerel or herrings, cleaned
with heads off**

**I small carrot
I pickled cucumber**

**FOR THE GARNISH
I pickled cucumber, sliced
dill sprigs**

1 Simmer the water, bay leaf, onion and seasoning for 10 minutes with a close-fitting lid on the pan. Add the vinegar and cool.

2 Bone the fish and cut each in half lengthwise to give 8 fillets.

3 Cut 8 thin sticks from the carrot and blanch them in boiling water for 1 minute. Drain and rinse under cold water. Cut 8 thin sticks lengthwise from the pickled cucumber. Place a stick of carrot and pickled cucumber at the wide end of each fish fillet and roll up to the tail, then secure with toothpicks. Place in the prepared, cooled liquid. Heat very gently until the liquid is steaming but not simmering. Cover and leave at this heat for 10 minutes. Remove from the heat and leave the fish to cool completely in the liquid. The rolls should be cooked through by the time they have cooled.

4 Lift the fish rolls from the cooking liquid when cool. Serve garnished with pickled cucumber and dill, whole or chopped.

Stuffed Fish Fillets with Egg and Lemon Sauce

[SERVES 6–8]

This is most certainly a dish for a special occasion. It takes a little longer than most, but it's well worth the effort for the delicious taste and excellent presentation.

6 tbsp. butter
2 garlic cloves, crushed
I onion, very finely chopped
½ green pepper, seeded and
very finely chopped
6 oz. shelled cooked shrimp,
roughly chopped
I cup fresh white bread crumbs
I tbsp. chopped fresh parsley

salt and freshly ground
black pepper
4 sole fillets, skinned
chopped fresh parsley, to garnish

FOR THE SAUCE
3 eggs
I ½ cups freshly squeezed
lemon juice
I ¼ cups warm fish stock

I Preheat the oven to 350°F. Melt 2 tbsp. of the butter in a large skillet. Sauté the garlic, onion and green pepper for about 5 minutes or until the onion is golden.

2 Add the shrimp to the onion mixture with the bread crumbs, parsley and salt and pepper and stir. Cook for a further minute, then remove from the heat. Cool slightly.

3 Divide the shrimp mixture between the fish fillets and spread evenly. Roll up the fillets and arrange them seam-side down in a large, buttered baking dish. Melt the remaining butter in a small saucepan and use to brush over the rolled fish fillets. Bake for 25–30 minutes, or until the fish flakes easily and is cooked through. Cut the rolls into ½-inch slices and arrange on a warm serving platter. Tent with aluminum foil to keep warm.

4 To make the egg and lemon sauce, beat the eggs in a medium-sized bowl and beat in the lemon juice, a little at a time. Very slowly beat in the warm fish stock. Pour the sauce into a small saucepan and gently heat, beating continuously, until slightly thickened. Pour over the fillets and sprinkle with a garnish of chopped parsley to serve.

Crab-stuffed Fish

[SERVES 4]

Use whole trout, red snapper, flounder or sole for this dish, cooked individually if you use small fish. Alternatively, present an elegant platter of a large, stuffed fish surrounded by lemon slices and parsley sprigs. If you use one large fish, a 2½- to 3-pound fish will serve 4–5 people. Fresh crab meat is best but frozen or canned are acceptable.

2 tbsp. butter
6 scallions, chopped
I ½ cups coarsely chopped
mushrooms
I tbsp. chopped fresh parsley
I clove garlic, finely chopped
¼ tsp. salt
¼ tsp. paprika
¼ tsp. black pepper
2 tbsp. grated Parmesan cheese

¼ cup heavy or light cream
½ lb. fresh crab meat,
picked over
4 whole fish, about ½ lb. each,
cleaned and boned
salt and freshly ground black
pepper to taste
flour for dredging (optional)
olive oil or melted butter

I Preheat the oven to 350°F. In a small skillet, melt the butter. Sauté the onions, mushrooms, parsley and garlic until limp, about 5 minutes. Stir in the salt, paprika, pepper, Parmesan and cream until well mixed. Add the crab, stirring gently. Set aside.

2 Rinse the fish and pat dry with paper towels. Season the insides lightly with salt and pepper. You may dredge the fish in flour at this point if you wish, covering the outside only with a thin coat of flour, and shaking off excess.

3 Stuff the fish with the crab mixture, then skewer it closed with toothpicks, or sew a few large stitches with strong thread. Put the fish in a lightly oiled baking pan and brush with olive oil or drizzle with melted butter.

4 Bake the fish until the flesh at the thickest point is opaque but still juicy, about 10 minutes. Do not wait for the fish to flake easily, because it continues cooking after it is removed from the oven, and would be overcooked by the time you serve it.

Fish and Vegetable Casserole

[SERVES 8–10]

Cod, haddock or monkfish are each suitable types of fish to use for this dish, which originates from the Greek island of Corfu. The crucial ingredient is the garlic, and plenty of it.

7 tbsp. olive oil
I large onion, sliced
2 lb. small new potatoes,
washed and cut into ½-inch slices
2 carrots, cut into I-inch chunks
I celery stick, chopped
salt and freshly ground
black pepper

6 garlic cloves, crushed
2½ lb, firm white fish fillets,
skinned and cut into 2-inch chunks
¼ cup freshly squeezed
lemon juice

1 Heat 4 tbsp. of the olive oil in a large, heavy-based saucepan and sauté the onion for about 3 minutes, or until softened.

2 Add the potatoes, carrots and celery, and season with salt and freshly ground black pepper. Continue to cook for a further 4–5 minutes, or until the vegetables begin to soften.

3 Stir in the garlic and pour over enough boiling water to just cover the vegetables. Bring to a boil, cover, and simmer for 10–15 minutes or until the vegetables are almost tender.

4 Gently stir the fish into the casserole, cover and simmer for 10–15 minutes or until the fish flakes easily, adding a little extra water if necessary. Just before the end of the cooking time, remove the cover and stir in the lemon juice and the remaining olive oil. Adjust the seasoning if necessary and serve.

Fresh Tuna Braised Bordelais Style

[SERVES 4]

5 tbsp. butter	**⅔ cup white wine**
4 tbsp. olive oil	**⅔ cup fish stock (see page 18)**
1 lb. fresh tuna	**3 cups mushrooms**
1 large onion	**salt and pepper**
5 medium tomatoes	

1 Amalgamate 4 tbsp. butter and the oil over a medium heat. Brown the fish in the oil and butter on both sides – about 2 minutes per side. Thinly slice the onion and add to the fish.

2 As the onion is cooking, seed and then dice the tomatoes. Add them to the mixture, together with the white wine and the fish stock. Bring the liquid to a boil, then lower the heat to a gentle simmer.

3 Cook the fish for 15 minutes, retrieve from the pan juices and set aside to keep warm.

4 With the remaining 1 tbsp. butter, fry the mushrooms until golden and add them to the pan juices. Turn up the heat and reduce by one-third. When the liquor is reduced, check the seasoning, pour over the tuna and serve immediately.

Fish Steaks with Mussels

[SERVES 4]

4 large firm, white fish steaks
seasoned flour
⅔ cup virgin olive oil
2 lb. ripe tomatoes
(or 2 × 14-oz. cans chopped
tomatoes), peeled and chopped
I large Spanish onion, chopped

4 large cloves garlic, chopped
½ cup unsalted butter, cubed
7 tbsp. dry white wine
2½ cups mussels, cleaned and
bearded
2½ cups rice, cooked "al dente"
chopped fresh parsley

I Dip the fish steaks in seasoned flour and fry them in 2 tbsp. of olive oil. Keep warm.

2 Cook the tomatoes, onion and garlic in the remainder of the olive oil and ¼ cup butter. Add the white wine and simmer for a while.

3 Discard any opened mussels. Add the cleaned mussels and cover with a lid. Cook over a high heat until the mussels have opened, shaking the pan from time to time during the cooking. Take off the flame and remove the mussels and keep with the fish. Discard any mussels that are closed. Put the pan back on the heat and reduce the sauce a little.

4 Add the rest of the butter cubes and beat until melted, then add the cooked rice and heat through. Shake the pan again while heating.

5 Put the fish steaks on a serving dish and cover with the mixture. Arrange the mussels in their shells on top and garnish with chopped parsley.

Seabass with Fennel Seeds in Pernod

[SERVES 4–6]

This is a quick, simple and impressive dinner-party dish. A whole fish such as trout can be substituted for the seabass.

I½ cups fresh bread crumbs
I egg
2 tsp. fennel seeds
salt and freshly ground
black pepper
2½ lb. seabass,
cleaned and scaled

I tsp. oil
4 tbsp. Pernod

FOR THE GARNISH
lemon
parsley

I Preheat the oven to 350°F. Mix together the bread crumbs, egg, fennel seeds and seasoning.

2 Fill the body cavity of the fish with the stuffing, then brush with oil. Place the fish in a baking dish and bake for 30 minutes until the fish is tender.

3 Place the fish on a serving dish. Heat the Pernod in a small pan, light and pour over the fish.

4 Garnish with lemon and parsley to serve.

Baked Seabass with Mayonnaise

[SERVES 6]

I seabass (about 2½ lb.),
cleaned and scaled
2 large onions, very finely sliced
4 tbsp. olive oil
2 cloves garlic, crushed
2 sprigs fresh rosemary
2 tbsp. finely chopped
fresh parsley

2 tbsp. finely chopped fresh basil
juice of I lemon
4 tbsp. dry white wine
salt and freshly ground
black pepper
2½ cups mayonnaise
(see page 20)

1 Preheat the oven to 350°F.

2 Make a fish-shaped bed of onion on a large piece of foil. Pour the olive oil over it and lay the fish on top.

3 Smear the garlic along the inside of the fish and lay the sprigs of rosemary in there, too. Mix the parsley and basil with the lemon juice, and similarly anoint the inside of the fish. Raise the edges of the foil, pour the white wine over and season. Seal the package carefully, making sure there are no holes or tears.

4 Set the foil package in an amply-sized dish and bake for 30 minutes. When ready, remove from the oven, but do not unseal until the package is completely cool. In the meantime, make the mayonnaise.

5 About 45 minutes before eating, remove the fish from its wrapper and collect all the juices into a small saucepan. Boil them down and leave to cool, then add them to the mayonnaise.

6 Decorate the fish with the onions on which it lay and serve.

Seabass Cooked with Seaweed in a Paper Case

[SERVES 6]

3 lb. seabass, cleaned
salt and pepper
I tbsp. each of fennel, shallots and
chopped fresh herbs
I lb. fresh seaweed
7 tbsp. dry white wine

FOR THE SAUCE
I sweet red pepper
I bulb of fennel

2 tomatoes (plum type, if
available), peeled and chopped
2 tbsp. chopped fresh herbs –
parsley, chives, chervil, fennel
and tarragon
lemon juice
olive oil
salt and pepper

1 Preheat the oven to 400°F. Season the seabass.

2 Place the chopped fennel, shallots and herbs in the middle of the fish. Wrap the fish in fresh seaweed and put in a package of parchment paper. Before you close the paper package, sprinkle the seabass with the white wine. Place on a baking sheet in the oven for about 30 minutes.

3 While the fish is cooking, make the sauce. Roast the pepper under the broiler, then peel and chop it finely. Chop the fennel into small pieces and combine with the tomatoes, pepper and herbs in a bowl. Mix well and add some lemon juice, olive oil and salt and pepper.

4 Serve the fish hot on a bed of seaweed with the sauce in a separate bowl.

Fried Swordfish with Almonds

[SERVES 4]

*This can be made with any firm, lean fish steaks, but as swordfish
becomes more widely available, it is well worth seeking out.*

**4 swordfish steaks
a little chili powder
salt**

**½ cup flaked almonds
3 tbsp. butter
2 tbsp. lime juice**

1 Dust the fish steaks with chili powder and salt to taste.

2 Fry the almonds in the butter for a couple of minutes until golden.
Drain and reserve.

3 Fry the fish steaks for 4 minutes each side, then add the lime juice,
cover, and cook for 10 minutes more.

4 Serve on rice, topped with the almonds and with the pan juices
poured over.

Braised Swordfish with Peppers

[SERVES 4]

**4 swordfish steaks
(about 6 oz. each)
4 tbsp. olive oil
4 cloves garlic
I medium onion, roughly chopped
I medium red pepper, seeded
and finely sliced**

**¼ lb. fresh or canned plum
tomatoes, roughly chopped
I chili pepper
⅔ cup dry white wine
salt and pepper to taste**

I Wash and thoroughly dry the steaks. Heat the oil over a high heat and seal each steak on each side.

2 Remove the fish from the pan and set it aside. Turn down the heat to medium and add the whole cloves of garlic and the onions.

3 Turn the heat once more to high and cook the onions until the edges begin to catch. Reduce the flame to a gentle simmer and cook until the onions and garlic are softened.

4 When the onions are soft, add the pepper and cook until it begins to soften – about 5 minutes. Add the tomatoes, the whole chili and the wine. Bring to a fierce boil, then add the fish. Turn the heat to a low simmer and cover the pan. Simmer until the fish is very tender, about 15 minutes.

5 Remove the fish from the pan and set it aside in a warm place. Boil up the pan juices very briskly until they are reduced to a thick, creamy mixture. Season, pour around the fish and serve.

Malaysian Fish Curry

[SERVES 6]

3½ cups shredded coconut
1¼ cups water, boiling
1½ lb. firm white fish, skinned and boned
salt and pepper
2 large onions, chopped
2 cloves garlic, chopped
1 tsp. ground coriander
½ tsp. ground cumin
½ tsp. ground turmeric
1 tsp. sugar

3–4 dried red chilies, soaked in hot water, or 1–1½ tsp. chili powder
½ tbsp. tamarind pulp soaked in 4 tbsp. hot water for 20 minutes, then squeezed out and discarded, or 4 tbsp. lime juice
3 tbsp. oil
2 tbsp. anchovy paste or blachan (Oriental fish paste)

1 First make coconut milk by putting the shredded coconut in a deep bowl and pouring the boiling water over. Leave to stand for 15 minutes, then squeeze out the liquid. Discard the coconut and leave the milk in the refrigerator until needed.

2 Chop the fish into bite-sized pieces and season.

3 In a blender, food processor or mortar, combine the onions, garlic, coriander, cumin, turmeric, sugar, dried chilies or chili powder and tamarind or lime juice and reduce to a thick paste. You may have to do this in 2 batches.

4 Fry the mixture in the oil for a couple of minutes, then add the anchovy paste or blachan and cook for a further minute.

5 Add the fish and coconut milk and simmer gently (do not boil) for 7–10 minutes, or until the fish is done.

6 Correct the seasoning and serve hot with plain boiled rice.

Brochettes of Monkfish with Basil and Orange

[SERVES 4]

2 lb. monkfish
2 oranges
⅔ cup olive oil
1 tbsp. finely chopped fresh basil

½ cup fresh bread crumbs
salt and freshly ground black pepper

1 Skin the monkfish and dice it into 2-inch square chunks.

2 Squeeze the juice from the oranges. Cut the peels into chunks about the size of the monkfish pieces and reserve. Combine the olive oil, the orange juice and the basil.

3 Add the fish to the marinade and scatter with the pieces of orange peel. Marinade for up to 2 hours.

4 Preheat the broiler to its maximum heat. Thread the fish onto skewers, alternating the pieces whenever you can with pieces of orange peel.

5 Brush liberally with the marinade once more. Sprinkle the side you are broiling first with half the bread crumbs. Broil for 6–7 minutes. Turn, bread crumb the other side, and broil again. Remove the brochettes to a serving platter.

6 Combine any pan juices with what remains of the marinade. Bring to a rapid boil, season and pour over the fish.

Fish Kabobs

[SERVES 6]

4 onions, roughly chopped
juice of 3 lemons
¼ cup olive oil
large pinch of cayenne pepper
2 tsp. cumin
1 tbsp. tomato paste
2 bay leaves
2 lb. fillet of seabass, cut into
1-inch cubes

18–24 cherry tomatoes
6 baby zucchini, trimmed,
scrubbed and cut into 3–4 pieces
each
olive oil
lemon wedges

1 Using a garlic press, squeeze the juice from the onion pieces a little at a time, until you have extracted as much as you can. In a bowl, mix the onion juice with the lemon juice and beat in the oil, cayenne to taste, cumin and tomato paste. Add the bay leaves.

2 Place the cubed fish in a larger bowl and pour the marinade over it; toss the fish with your hands. Cover and leave to chill for 1 hour.

3 On 6 large or 12 small skewers, thread the fish cubes, baby zucchini and cherry tomatoes. Place under a preheated hot broiler and brush with a little oil, especially on the vegetables. Cook for 10–15 minutes, turning once or twice, until the fish is opaque and the zucchini are just tender. Serve immediately with lemon wedges and rice.

Baked Stuffed Fish

[SERVES 6]

This Lebanese recipe has many variations. The optional pomegranate seeds are an introduction from Iran, but one that is much appreciated in the Lebanon. If the stuffed fish is white-fleshed, it is often served cold; if it is an oily fish, it is always served hot, simply garnished with lemon wedges.

4 lb. seabass or mullet, cleaned and scaled (or 6 × 10-oz. whole mackerel)
olive oil
salt and freshly ground pepper
1 small onion, finely chopped
½ green pepper, finely chopped
1 cup pine nuts
½ tsp. bruised coriander seeds
½ cup fresh bread crumbs
2–3tsp golden raisins

2 tbsp. pomegranate seeds (optional)
5 tbsp. finely chopped flat-leaf parsley
4 tbsp. fresh lemon juice
lemon wedges

FOR THE GARNISH
cucumber, olives, tomatoes, green peppers, pimento, anchovies, hard-boiled eggs, toasted pine nuts (optional)

1 If you are stuffing 1 whole white fish, rub it liberally with olive oil and rub in salt and pepper to taste. Leave to chill for 1 hour.

2 If using mackerel, do not buy the fish gutted; take them home whole. Sever the heads, leaving them attached by a small piece of skin. Snap the tail sharply, breaking the backbone inside the fish, and roll the fish back and forth to loosen the bone and flesh.

3 Using a spoon, scoop out the innards of the fish, and follow this by drawing out the loosened backbone. Use the spoon to press the flesh against the sides of the fish, enlarging the hole for stuffing. Wash the fish inside and out, pat dry and set aside.

4 To make the stuffing, heat 3 tbsp. olive oil. Sauté the onion for about 5 minutes over medium heat, stirring, until softened. Add the green pepper and continue stirring, until it is soft and the onions are

changing color. Stir in the pine nuts for another 2 minutes, then the crushed coriander seeds and bread crumbs. Stir for about 1 minute. Remove the pan from the heat and add the golden raisins, pomegranate seeds (if used) and the parsley. Season the stuffing with salt and pepper to taste, and moisten it with 1 tbsp. lemon juice.

5 Preheat the oven to 400°F. Stuff the large white fish or the smaller mackerel with the mixture. Secure the white fish with a little thread or small skewers; fill the mackerel through the top opening and replace the heads as well as possible. Arrange the fish on a baking sheet and pour over the remaining lemon juice (and more oil on the white fish, if this is necessary).

6 Place the fish in the oven and bake, covered loosely with foil, for 40–45 minutes for the whole fish, or about 30 minutes for the mackerel.

7 Remove from the oven. Serve the mackerel immediately with lemon wedges; the white fish may also be served hot or it may be left to cool.

8 In the latter case, the fish is usually garnished with paper-thin cucumber slices, olive rings, tomato roses with green pepper leaves, pimento and anchovy strips, slices of hard-boiled egg and toasted pine nuts.

Fish Bake

[SERVES 4]

This dish of cold cooked fish coated in sesame seed sauce and decorated with nuts and salad ingredients is popular in the Middle East. Tahini (sesame seed paste) is available in jars from grocery stores and health-food stores.

1 whole fish approximately 2½ lb. (such as seabass, trout, snapper), cleaned and scaled
1 tbsp. lemon juice
salt and freshly ground black pepper
1 tbsp. oil

½ cup tahini
1 clove garlic, crushed
2 tbsp. chopped fresh parsley

FOR THE GARNISH
olives, radishes, cucumber, pine nuts, lettuce, parsley, tomatoes and lemon

1 Preheat the oven to 400°F. Place the fish in a shallow baking dish and sprinkle the lemon juice and seasoning over.

Brush with oil, cover with aluminum foil and bake for 25–35 minutes until the fish is tender. Lift the fish on to a serving dish and chill.

2 In a bowl, mix together the tahini, garlic and parsley. Add a little water if the mixture is too thick to spread.

3 Spread over the fish and garnish with the olives, radishes, cucumber, pine nuts, lettuce, parsley, tomatoes and lemon.

Fish Bake (top right)

Stuffed Red Mullet (bottom)

Stuffed Red Mullet

[SERVES 4]

Use trout for this Mediterranean dish if red mullet are unavailable.

¼ cup long-grain rice
4 red mullet or trout
½ tsp. turmeric
I clove garlic, crushed
I chili, seeded and
finely chopped
2 tbsp. chopped fresh parsley
3 tbsp. pine nuts

6 ripe olives, pitted and chopped
2 tbsp. lemon juice
salt and freshly ground
black pepper
2 tbsp. vegetable oil
4 lemon slices
4 fresh parsley sprigs
lemon, to garnish

I Preheat the oven to 375°F. Place the rice in a large saucepan. Cover with water, bring to a boil and simmer for 15 minutes. Drain.

2 Make a slit in the belly of each fish and remove the insides. Wash and dry.

3 In a bowl, mix together the turmeric, garlic, chili, parsley, pine nuts, rice, olives, lemon juice and seasoning. Use to stuff the fish.

4 Place each fish on a piece of aluminum foil. Brush the fish with oil and top each with a slice of lemon and a sprig of parsley. Wrap the foil like a package around the fish and lift onto a baking sheet.

5 Bake for 30 minutes or until the fish is cooked and tender. Remove from the foil and lift carefully onto a serving dish. Garnish with lemon and serve with salad.

Baked Fish

[SERVES 4–6]

I garlic clove, crushed
juice of ½ lemon
½ cup olive oil
2 tsp. dried oregano
salt and freshly ground
black pepper

I whole seabass, or 2–3 whole red
mullet or trout, depending on size
lemon wedges (optional)

I In a small bowl, mash the garlic into the lemon juice until you have a paste. Beat in the olive oil until emulsified, then add the oregano and seasoning to taste.

2 Place the fish on a large piece of foil, and pour some of the

marinade over it. Rub it into the fish on both sides. Close the foil over the fish, and chill for 1–2 hours.

3 Preheat the oven to 350°F. Open the foil, pour a little more marinade over, and seal again. Place on a baking sheet and cook for 40–50 minutes, depending on the number and size of the fish. Test by inserting a knife or skewer into the flesh of the fish; it should be opaque.

4 Serve hot with lemon wedges, or cold.

Fillets of Turbot with Cucumbers

[SERVES 4]

1½ tbsp. finely chopped shallot
salt and freshly ground
white pepper
4 turbot fillets, approximately
6 oz. each cut into 3
⅓ cup dry white wine
6 tbsp. fish stock
½ large firm straight cucumber
¼ cup dry vermouth

⅔ cup heavy cream
3 tbsp. butter, diced
a squeeze of lemon juice
½ tsp. finely chopped tarragon

FOR THE GARNISH
small sprigs of tarragon
lemon

1 Scatter the shallots over a large, buttered flameproof dish. Season the turbot and lay the slices side by side on the shallots. Heat the wine and stock, then pour over the turbot. Cover with buttered foil. Bring just to a boil, lower the heat and poach for 5 minutes.

2 Cut the cucumber in half lengthwise, scoop out the seeds and "turn" the flesh (see page 65) so that each piece is backed by green skin. Blanch, refresh and drain well.

3 Carefully transfer the fish to a warmed plate, cover and keep warm.

4 Add the vermouth to the poaching liquid and reduce by a quarter. Stir in the cream and boil until slightly thickened. Pass through a strainer and reheat gently. Gradually swirl in 2 tbsp. butter, making sure each piece is fully incorporated before adding the next. Season and add a squeeze of lemon juice. Keep warm but do not boil.

5 Heat the remaining tbsp. butter. Stir in the tarragon, add the cucumber and heat through gently, shaking the pan frequently. Carefully remove with a slotted spoon.

6 Spoon the sauce over 4 warmed plates, carefully arrange the fish on top, add the cucumber and garnish with the sprigs of tarragon and lemon.

Turbot with Tomatoes and Mushrooms

[SERVES 4]

⅔ cup good-quality sparkling
dry white wine
⅔ cup Madeira wine
1 cup fish stock
2 tbsp. very finely chopped
shallots
3 tomatoes, peeled, seeded and
chopped

3 cups sliced button mushrooms
4 fillets of turbot, each
approximately 6 oz.
salt and freshly ground
black pepper
1 cup heavy cream
2 tbsp. finely chopped fresh
parsley

1 Heat the sparkling wine, Madeira wine and stock to simmering point in a saucepan or flameproof dish that is large enough to hold the fish in a single layer. Add the shallots, tomatoes and mushrooms, reduce the heat so the liquid is just moving, then lay the fillets on the vegetables. Season, cover the fish with buttered parchment paper and poach for 4 minutes.

2 Carefully transfer the fish to a warmed plate, cover and keep warm.

3 Boil the liquid until reduced to about 6 tbsp. Stir in the cream and any juices that have come out of the fish and boil until the sauce is slightly thickened, stirring frequently.

4 Divide the sauce between 4 warmed plates and arrange a bed of vegetables on one half of each plate. Sprinkle the parsley over the borders of the "beds" and the surrounding sauce then place the fillets on the "beds."

Turbot with Leeks and Mushroom Mélange

[SERVES 6]

Choose dishes that do not require much last-minute preparation to serve before and after this dish. Just a simple vegetable is all that is needed to accompany it.

12 young leeks, white parts only
salt and freshly ground
white pepper
6 turbot fillets, each
approximately 5 oz.
3 tbsp. lemon juice
15 tbsp. butter, diced
2 shallots, finely chopped
1 ¼ cups dry white wine
1 ½ cups finely chopped button
mushrooms

10 oz. chanterelles, morels or
mousserons
2 tbsp. truffle juice (optional)
2 tbsp. Madeira wine (or
4 tbsp. if truffle juice is not used)
2 tbsp. whipping cream
1 tbsp. finely snipped fresh chives

1 Preheat the oven to 400°F.

2 Blanch the leeks for 3–4 minutes. Refresh, drain well, then cut into ½-inch slices.

3 Season the turbot and sprinkle with some of the lemon juice.

4 Heat 1 tbsp. butter in a skillet large enough to hold the turbot fillets in one layer. Add the shallots and cook over a moderate heat until soft. Stir in the wine and boil for 1 minute. Add the button mushrooms and place the turbot on top. Place a piece of buttered parchment paper on the fish, put on the lid and put in the oven for 3 minutes.

5 Meanwhile, melt 1 tbsp. butter. Add the wild mushrooms and cook for 2–3 minutes. Add a squeeze of lemon juice and the truffle juice (if using), and cook for 1 minute. Remove the mushrooms with a slotted spoon, cover and keep warm.

6 Stir the Madeira wine into the mushroom juices and reduce until syrupy. Reduce the heat to very low and gradually beat in 1 tbsp. butter.

7 Gently warm the slices of leek in 1 tbsp. butter and a very little water in a small covered pan.

8 Lift the turbot from the skillet, cover and keep warm. Pass the juices through a fine strainer, pressing hard to extract as much flavor as possible, then boil until reduced by one-third. Stir in the cream, bring to a boil and gradually beat in the remaining butter at a full boil. Add the chives, seasoning and lemon juice to taste. Keep warm, but do not boil.

9 Place a turbot fillet in the center of each warmed plate and arrange small mounds of leeks and small circles of dark sauce alternately around the fish. Place small mounds of mushrooms on the sauce. Pour the white wine sauce over the fish.

Coriander Baked Fish

[SERVES 4]

I tbsp. ground coriander	finely grated peel and juice of
pinch of chili powder	small orange
½ tsp. ground allspice	I ½ lb. fillet of white fish,
I tbsp. oil	skinned, or a whole fish
I cup thick plain yogurt	2–3 tbsp. chopped fresh cilantro

I Fry the spices in the oil for a minute or so to release the flavors. Off the heat, stir in the yogurt and orange peel and juice.

2 Deeply score the fish and put it in a baking dish. Mask with the yogurt mixture. Cover and leave to marinate for 2–3 hours.

3 Preheat the oven to 350°F. Bake the fish, still in its yogurt coating, for 30–35 minutes, depending on thickness.

4 Serve hot, sprinkled with fresh cilantro.

Skewered Fish

[SERVES 4]

2–3 dried red chillies	2 small bananas (not too ripe)
juice of 2 limes	lime wedges
15ml/1tbsp oil	
450g/1lb firm white fish, filleted	
and skinned	

I Soak the chillies in hot water for 30 minutes, then rinse them, chop very finely and mix with half the lime juice and the oil.

2 Chop the fish into 2.5cm/1in chunks and arrange them in a single layer on a plate. Pour the chilli mixture over them and leave to marinate in a cool place (not the refrigerator) for 1–2 hours.

3 Peel the bananas, cut them into 10mm/⅓in slices and sprinkle with the rest of the lime juice.

4 Thread the marinated fish cubes on to flat skewers, alternating with banana slices.

5 Grill or barbecue, turning frequently and basting with the remaining marinade, until the fish is just cooked.

6 Serve immediately, with plain rice, a green salad and lime wedges.

Haddock in Sweet-and-Sour Sauce

[SERVES 2–4]

Serve this dish with fluffy white rice.

I tbsp. minced onion	7-oz. can tomatoes,
I clove garlic, crushed	drained and strained
2 hot chilies, seeded and	I tbsp. tomato paste
finely sliced	a pinch of sugar
I slice fresh ginger root, grated	finely shredded scallions
3 tbsp. sherry	tomato slices
4 haddock fillets, weighing about	
I lb. in total	

I For the marinade, mix together in a microwave-safe dish the onion, garlic, chilies, ginger and sherry. Lay the fish in the marinade and leave for 1 hour, turning occasionally.

2 Mix together the tomatoes, tomato paste and sugar and pour over the fish. Cover with vented plastic wrap and cook on Full for about 5 minutes, until done, turning once.

3 Serve garnished with finely shredded scallions and tomato slices.

Fish in Vermouth Sauce

[SERVES 4]

Use any white fish fillets for this recipe.

I tbsp. oil	⅔ cup light cream
I shallot, chopped	salt
I cup wiped and sliced	cayenne pepper
mushrooms	4 fillets white fish
2 tbsp. dry vermouth	a little butter

I First make the sauce. Put the oil in a microwave-safe dish and cook on Full for 30 seconds. Add the shallot and cook on Full for 2 minutes. Add the mushrooms and vermouth, cover with vented plastic wrap and cook on Full for 3 minutes, stirring once.

2 Stir in the cream and season to taste with salt and cayenne pepper.

3 Put the fish fillets in a microwave-safe dish and dot with butter. Cover with vented plastic wrap and cook on Full for 3–4 minutes.

4 Heat the sauce through for 1 minute.

5 Lay the fish fillets on heated plates, pour the sauce over and serve.

Fillets of Cod with Caper Sauce

[SERVES 4]

3 tbsp. butter	2 tsp. vinegar from the caper jar
⅓ cup all-purpose flour	salt and pepper
1 ¼ cups milk	4 cod fillets
2 tbsp. capers, chopped	a little butter

I First make the sauce. Put the butter in a microwave-safe bowl and cook on Full for 45 seconds. Stir in the flour. Pour in the milk and cook on Full for 3 minutes, beating after each minute. Stir in the capers and vinegar and season to taste with salt and pepper.

2 Put the cod fillets in a microwave-safe dish and dot with butter. Cover with vented plastic wrap and cook on Full for 3–4 minutes, turning once.

3 Put the cod on heated plates, pour the sauce over and serve.

Fillets of Mackerel with Cranberry Sauce

Fillets of Mackerel with Cranberry Sauce

[SERVES 4]

2 large mackerel	salt and freshly ground
1⅓ cups cranberries	black pepper
2 tbsp. lemon juice	radicchio leaves
1 tbsp. Port wine	

1 Fillet the fish. Gut the mackerel, cut off the fins and carefully remove the bone from the head downward. Cut off the heads. Remove the skin and the remaining bones.

2 Make the sauce. Combine the cranberries, lemon juice and Port wine in a microwave-safe bowl and season with salt and pepper. Cook on Full for 4 minutes, until the berries are soft. Keep warm.

3 Lay the fish in a shallow microwave-safe dish, cover with vented plastic wrap and cook on Full for 4 minutes, turning once.

4 Arrange the mackerel fillets on a bed of radicchio leaves on heated plates, pour the sauce over and serve.

Soused Herring

[SERVES 4]

1 tbsp. oil	1 tbsp. pickling spices
1 onion, cut into rings	1 bay leaf
1 large apple, peeled, cored and sliced	⅔ cup cider vinegar
	4 herring, cleaned and boned

1 Put the oil in a microwave-safe dish and cook on Full for 30 seconds. Add the onion and cook on Full for 2 minutes.

2 Mix the onion with the apple, add the pickling spices and bay leaf and pour the cider vinegar over. Lay the herring on top. Cover with vented plastic wrap. Cook on Full until the vinegar boils and then for about 3 more minutes, until the fish are done. Leave to cool.

3 Serve the fish cold with a spoonful of the cooking vinegar and apple and onion slices on top.

Monkfish, Cauliflower and Snow Peas

[SERVES 4]

This is a very popular dish in Singapore, where it is served with a bowl of
rice.

½ cauliflower
2 tbsp. water
¾ lb. snow peas
¾ lb. monkfish pieces (or other
firm white fish, such as grouper)

2 tbsp. dry sherry
2 tbsp. soy sauce
I clove garlic, crushed

I Break the cauliflower into flowerets, discarding tough stems and leaves. Put it in a microwave-safe bowl with the water, cover and cook on Full for 3–4 minutes, until you can pierce the stems with the point of a sharp knife. Stir once during cooking.

2 String the snow peas. Put the cauliflower and peas in a microwave-safe bowl with the monkfish.

3 Combine the sherry, soy sauce and garlic. Pour over the vegetables and monkfish, stirring well. Leave for 30 minutes to marinate, stirring occasionally.

4 Cover the bowl with vented plastic wrap and cook on Full for 3 minutes, stirring once. Serve immediately.

Monkfish and Baby Leeks in Cheese Sauce

[SERVES 4]

14 oz. monkfish (or any other
firm white fish, such as grouper),
skinned and cut into pieces
8 baby leeks, washed and trimmed
2–3 tbsp. water
3 tbsp. butter

⅓ cup all-purpose flour
1 ¼ cups milk
⅓ cup grated Parmesan cheese
salt and freshly ground
black pepper

I Put the monkfish (or equivalent) and leeks in a large, oblong microwave-safe dish and add the water. Cover with vented plastic wrap and cook on Full for 5 minutes, rearranging once, until the fish is done and the leeks are tender. Set aside while you make the sauce.

2 Put the butter in a microwave-safe measuring jug and cook on Full for 45 seconds. Stir in the flour. Pour in the milk and cook on Full for 3 minutes, beating after each minute. Stir in the cheese and cook on Full for a further minute. Beat again. Season to taste.

3 Pour the sauce over the leeks and monkfish and heat through before serving.

Monkfish, Cauliflower and Snow Peas

Herrings with Horseradish Sauce

[SERVES 4]

3 egg yolks
3 tbsp. white-wine vinegar
6 tbsp. butter, diced
1½ oz. horseradish, peeled and
grated

salt and freshly ground
white pepper
4 herrings, whole or filleted

1 Beat the egg yolks with the wine vinegar. Put the butter in a microwave-safe bowl and cook on Full for 1½ minutes until melted. Beat the yolks and vinegar into the butter. Cook on Full for 30 seconds.

2 Beat again, adding the horseradish gradually. Beat until cool and thick. Season with salt and white pepper. Set aside.

3 Put the herrings in a microwave-safe dish, cover with vented plastic wrap and cook on Full for 3–4 minutes, until done, turning once.

4 Arrange the herrings on 4 heated plates. Serve with green beans, if liked, and the horseradish sauce.

Fish Curry

[SERVES 4]

1½ lb. cod, skinned and cubed
⅔ cup plain yogurt
1 tsp. turmeric
1 clove garlic, crushed

3 tbsp. butter
1 large onion, finely sliced
5 cardamom pods
3 cloves

1 Put the fish in a dish. Mix together the yogurt, turmeric and garlic and stir into the fish. Leave to marinate for 1 hour.

2 Put the butter in a large microwave-safe dish and cook on Full for 45 seconds. Add the onions and spices, cover and cook on Full for 3 minutes.

3 Stir in the fish and marinade, cover and cook on Medium for 10 minutes, stirring once. Serve with rice.

Herrings with Horseradish Sauce

Sole with Sage and Butter

[SERVES 2]

2 whole sole, skinned, each weighing 8–10 oz.	salt and freshly ground black pepper
8 sage leaves	lemon wedges
2 tbsp. butter, diced	

1 Lay the sole in a microwave-safe dish with the sage leaves and dot with butter. Cover with vented plastic wrap and cook on Full for about 3 minutes, turning the dish once. As sole is so delicate, it is better to undercook and add on a few seconds if it is still not done.

2 When the fish is ready, transfer to heated plates. Season with salt and pepper and serve with lemon wedges.

Red Mullet with Ham

[SERVES 4]

4 red mullet, cleaned	FOR THE GARNISH
4 slices cooked ham	fresh herbs
a little butter	12 thin slices of zucchini cooked
⅔ cup light cream	for 30 seconds
½ tbsp. tomato paste	

1 Lay the mullet on the ham in a greased microwave-safe dish. Dot with butter. Cover with vented plastic wrap and cook on Full for 3–4 minutes, turning once.

2 Mix the cream with the tomato paste in a bowl and cook for 1 minute on Medium.

3 Spoon the sauce onto 4 heated plates. Put the ham slices in the sauce and the mullets on top. Garnish each serving with fresh herbs and 3 zucchini slices.

Crispy Whiting Fillets

[SERVES 4]

8 whiting fillets	dried bread crumbs
salt and freshly ground	I tbsp. oil
black pepper	2 tbsp. butter
2 eggs, beaten	lemon slices

1 Sprinkle the whiting with salt and pepper. Dip in beaten egg and then in the bread crumbs, pressing them on well to cover the fish.

2 Heat a browning dish to maximum, according to the manufacturer's directions. Add the oil and butter. Cook on Full for 30 seconds. Protecting your hands with oven mitts, tilt the dish so it is well oiled.

3 Lay the whiting fillets in the dish (cook them in 2 batches if necessary) and cook for 4 minutes, turning once.

4 Serve with lemon slices and wholewheat bread and butter and a salad if liked.

Crispy Whiting Fillets

Fish with Fennel Sauce

[SERVES 4]

Fennel goes particularly well with fish. Use any white fish in this recipe.

½ fennel bulb, chopped
2 tbsp. water
3 tbsp. butter
⅓ cup all-purpose flour
1 ¼ cups milk
salt and pepper
4 fillets white fish
a little butter
chopped fennel leaves, to garnish

1 First make the sauce. Put the fennel in a microwave-safe dish with the water. Cover with vented plastic wrap and cook on Full for 5 minutes, until tender, stirring once. Set aside.

2 Put the butter in a microwave-safe bowl and cook on Full for 30 seconds. Stir in the flour. Pour in the milk and cook on Full for 3 minutes, beating after each minute. Stir in the fennel and season with salt and pepper. Keep warm.

3 Cook the fish. Put the fillets in a microwave-safe dish and dot with butter. Cover with vented plastic wrap and cook for 3–4 minutes until done.

4 Lay the fillets on heated plates. Pour the sauce over and garnish with chopped fennel leaves.

Anchovy and Potato Bake

[SERVES 4]

3 tbsp. butter
1 large onion, finely sliced
2 lb. potatoes, peeled and
coarsely grated
2-oz. canned anchovies, drained,
soaked in milk for 30 minutes,
then dried and chopped
2 tbsp. capers
cayenne pepper
⅔ cup light cream
3 tbsp. grated Parmesan cheese

1 Put the butter in a microwave-safe dish and cook on Full for 45 seconds. Add the onion, cover and cook on Full for 3 minutes.

2 Mix in the potatoes, cover and cook on Full for 8 minutes, until soft.

3 Stir in the anchovies and capers and season with cayenne pepper. Pour in the cream and top with grated Parmesan cheese. Cook on Medium for 4 minutes, until hot through.

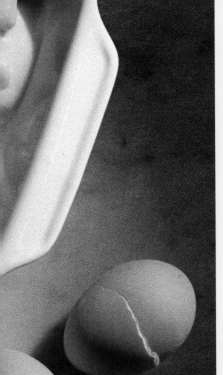

Fisherman's Pie

[SERVES 4]

1 ½ lb. smoked cod or haddock
fillets, skinned
1 ½ cups mushrooms
4 small leeks, sliced
1 ¼ cups milk
3 tbsp. butter
⅓ cup all-purpose flour
⅓ cup grated Gruyère cheese
⅓ cup grated Parmesan cheese
salt and freshly ground
black pepper
2 hard-boiled eggs, sliced
½ lb. shelled cooked shrimp
3 cups mashed potatoes
with plenty of butter
and a little milk

1 Put the fish fillets in a deep, oval microwave-safe dish with the mushrooms and leeks and add about 4 tbsp. of the milk. Cover and cook on Full for 3–4 minutes until the fish is tender. Pour off the milk and reserve. Flake the fish with a fork.

2 Put the butter in a microwave-safe measuring jug or bowl and cook on Full for 1 minute, until melted. Stir in the flour. Cook on Full for 1 minute. Pour in the milk the fish was cooked in and the remaining milk. Cook on Full for 3 minutes, beating the sauce after each minute. Add the cheeses and season. Cook on Full for a further minute and beat again.

3 Combine the fish, mushrooms, leeks, eggs and shrimp in the dish and stir in the sauce. Top with the mashed potato and heat through on Full for about 4 minutes.

4 Brown the top under the broiler if liked before serving.

Haddock and Vegetables
on a Bed of Noodles

[SERVES 4]

3 tbsp. butter	7 oz. asparagus spears
⅓ cup all-purpose flour	7 oz. fava beans,
⅔ cup milk	cooked or canned
⅔ cup light cream	½ lb. fresh spinach tagliatelle
3 tbsp. grated Parmesan cheese	boiling water
l egg yolk	salt
4 haddock fillets, about 6 oz.	l tsp. oil
each, skinned	paprika
2–3 tbsp. milk	

I First make the sauce. Put the butter in a microwave-safe bowl and cook on Full for 1 minute. Stir in the flour and cook on Full for 1 minute. Stir in the milk and cook on Full for 2 minutes, beating after each minute. Stir in the cream and cheese and cook on Full for 2 minutes, beating after each minute. Stir in the egg yolk. Keep the sauce warm.

2 Put the haddock in a dish with the milk, asparagus spears and fava beans. Cover with vented plastic wrap and cook for 4 minutes, turning once, until the fish is done. Keep warm.

3 Put the tagliatelle in a pot and pour boiling water over to just cover. Add a pinch of salt and the oil, cover and cook on Full for 3–4 minutes, until al dente.

4 Pour pools of sauce onto 4 heated serving plates. Drain the noodles well and divide between the plates of sauce.

5 Flake the haddock on top of the noodles, dust with paprika and serve with the fava beans and asparagus spears.

Shellfish

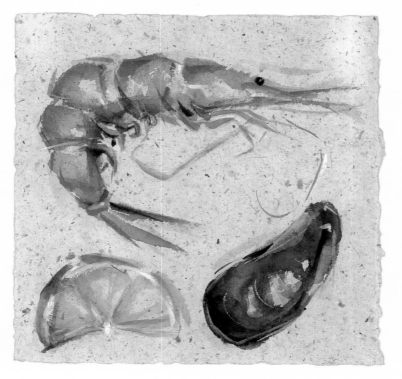

Because there is a high percentage of waste with shellfish it tends to be expensive and is looked upon as something of a treat. Nevertheless, its rich flavor makes it go far and, cooked judiciously, it can be more economical than might at first appear. Just a few shrimps make a tasty and different stir-fry, and dishes such as Seafood Jambalaya use rice to make a very filling meal. The main thing to remember about shellfish is that it should be very, very fresh.

Crown of Lobster and Scallops with Asparagus

[SERVES 4]

This is a very elegant-looking and tasting dish that is not at all
complicated. It is ideal for a summer dinner.

sprig fresh thyme
I shallot, chopped
¾ cup pink champagne or
other good-quality dry sparkling
rosé wine
I ¼ cups fish stock
½ cup heavy cream
¼ cup butter, diced
I tbsp. champagne vinegar
salt and freshly ground
white pepper

I2 scallops
½ cup dry white wine
flesh from 2 cooked lobster tails,
sliced
I2 green asparagus spears, sliced
on the diagonal

FOR THE GARNISH
crayfish tails
slices of truffle

1 Bring the thyme, shallot, champagne and stock to a boil and reduce by three-quarters. Pass through a fine strainer, return to the rinsed-out pan, stir in the cream and simmer for 5 minutes. Reduce the heat to very low and gradually beat in 2 tbsp. butter, making sure that each piece is completely incorporated before adding the next. Stir in the vinegar. Season and keep warm, but do not let boil.

2 Remove the scallops from their shells and separate the corals from the bodies. Slice the bodies in half horizontally.

3 Heat the wine, season lightly, add the scallop bodies and slices of lobster tail and poach for about 1 minute. Turn them over, add the corals and poach for a further minute.

4 Meanwhile, steam the slices of asparagus for about 5 minutes.

5 Spoon the sauce over 4 warmed plates. Remove the fish from the wine with a slotted spoon and arrange on the sauce in a circle like a crown. Arrange the asparagus in the centers and garnish with crayfish tails and slices of truffle.

Jamaican Broiled Lobster

[SERVES 4]

2 cooked lobsters (best when
heavy for their size), weighing
about I ½ lb. each
a little oil
6 tbsp. butter
2 cloves garlic, finely crushed
2 tsp. mixed fresh herbs, or
I tsp. dried mixed herbs

2 pinches cayenne pepper
2 tbsp. finely chopped scallions
(green part only)
salt and pepper
2 tbsp. chopped fresh parsley
3 tbsp. fresh white bread crumbs

1 Split each lobster in half, leaving the head and small claws on. Remove the meat from the head and tail and discard the intestine, stomach and gills. Crack the claws carefully and extract the meat.

2 Cut the lobster meat into bite-sized pieces and brush the outsides of the shells with a little oil to keep them shiny.

3 Shortly before serving, melt 4 tbsp. of the butter over a low heat with the garlic and add the lobster meat, mixed herbs, cayenne, scallions and a little salt and pepper.

4 Heat the meat through gently for 2–3 minutes, shaking the pan from time to time. Pile back into the shells and top with the parsley and bread crumbs.

5 Dot with the remaining butter and cook under a hot, preheated broiler for 5–7 minutes, until the topping is crisp and golden. Serve immediately, accompanied by rum punch or beer.

Picture on page 132

Dublin Lawyer

[SERVES 2]

This is a traditional way to serve fresh lobster in Ireland. It is essential to make it with fresh lobster.

6 tbsp. butter
I fresh lobster, about
2½ lb., cut into chunks,
together with the coral

4 tbsp. Irish whiskey
⅔ cup heavy cream
salt and pepper

1 Melt the butter in a heavy pan until it froths, but do not brown it. Cook the lobster meat and the coral lightly for a few minutes.

2 Warm the whiskey, set it alight, and flame the lobster. When the flames die down, add the cream. Heat for a few moments – on no account let it boil.

3 Place the meat and sauce back into the lobster shells. Serve on a bed of chilled lettuce or on a bed of boiled rice.

Broiled Lobster with Red Butter Sauce

[SERVES 4]

*If killing a live lobster as described is too daunting, ask the fish merchant
to do it for you, and to remove the stomach sac and intestine. But be sure
to have the lobster prepared on the day of cooking. Freshness is all.*

4 small live lobsters
cayenne pepper
unsalted butter, melted

FOR THE SAUCE
1 shallot, finely chopped
2 cups dry white wine
1 tsp fish glaze (see page 18)

½ cup unsalted butter, chilled
and cut into small lumps
coral from the lobster, if available
3 tbsp. heavy cream
1 tsp. tomato paste

FOR THE GARNISH
watercress

1 First prepare the butter sauce. Put the shallot into a small saucepan with the white wine. Cook slowly until the liquid is reduced by half. Strain into a clean pan. Add the fish glaze and set aside.

2 Next kill the lobsters (see right).

3 Lay the lobsters out flat and split in half lengthwise. Remove the stomach sac from near the head and the threadlike intestine.

4 Preheat the broiler. Brush the lobsters with butter and season with cayenne pepper. Place under the broiler, cut side uppermost first, for 8–10 minutes a side (depending on size) or until the lobsters are a good bright red.

5 While the lobsters are cooking, continue with the butter sauce. Mix 1 tsp. butter with the coral. Set aside.

6 When the lobsters are cooked, crack the claws (without removing from the body) in a claw-cracker or by covering with a cloth and hitting with a rolling pin. Keep the lobsters warm while finishing the sauce.

7 Warm up the reduced wine and fish glaze. Using a wire whisk and plenty of vigorous continuous whisking, add the butter bit by bit. The process should take 1½–2 minutes and the sauce should thicken considerably. Do not let it get too hot.

8 Whisk in the coral butter and cream, and any pan juices from the broiler. Add a little tomato paste to color. Season as required.

9 Arrange the lobsters on a large oval dish. Garnish with watercress and hand the sauce separately.

1 *To kill lobster for broiling, locate the well-defined cross on the back of the head.*

2 *Pierce firmly with a sharp, heavy knife. The lobster will die instantly, although it might still move alarmingly.*

3 *Continue the cut down the back to split the lobster in half lengthwise.*

4 *Turn it around and split the head.*

5 *Extract the cartilaginous stomach sac from near the head. It will probably have been split by the knife so look for the other half in the second half-shell.*

6 *Pull it away and discard it.*

7 *Pull away and discard the thin threadlike intestine (possibly in pieces) that runs from head to tail.*

8 *Scoop out the soft greeny-gray, or creamy, tomalley or liver if it is to be used in a sauce, or leave it in place for broiling. Do not discard – it is delicious. Remove the greeny-black roe, if any, to the sauce or leave in place if preferred. It turns bright red when cooked, and tastes excellent.*

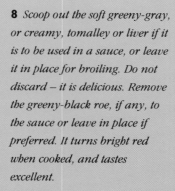

Creamed Crab

½ lb. freshly cooked crab meat
2 tomatoes, peeled and chopped
2 hard-boiled eggs, chopped
1 ¼ cups mayonnaise mixed with
½ tbsp. mixed fresh herbs
(basil, parsley, cilantro, chives)

juice of 1 lemon
chopped fresh chives and parsley
salt and pepper

1 Put all the ingredients in a bowl and mix well. Serve with chilled pieces of romaine lettuce, or in vol-au-vent cases.

Deviled Crab

[SERVES 4]

I crab per person (cooked)	I heaped tbsp. Dijon mustard
½ cup butter, melted	lemon juice
2 cups fresh bread crumbs	pinch of cayenne pepper

1 Preheat the oven to 350°F. Remove all the meat from the freshly cooked crabs.

2 Place the meat in a mixing bowl with the melted butter and fresh bread crumbs. Add the mustard, lemon juice and cayenne. Mix very well.

3 Stuff the mixture back into the crab shells and heat in a very hot oven for 15 minutes. Finish under the broiler for a few minutes more. Serve very hot with lemon wedges.

Crab Meat with Cream of Chinese Cabbage

[SERVES 4–6]

¾ lb. Chinese cabbage	2 slices fresh ginger root
3 tbsp. shortening	I tbsp. chopped white part of
salt and pepper to taste	scallion
5 tbsp. good stock (see page 18)	5–6 oz. crab meat
3 tbsp. vegetable oil	I tbsp. dry sherry or white wine

1 Cut the cabbage into ½- to 1-inch sections.

2 Heat the shortening in a wok or skillet. When hot, stir-fry the cabbage for 1 minute. Sprinkle with salt and pepper to taste and add 3 tbsp. stock. Stir-fry for 1½ minutes. Transfer to a heated dish.

3 Reheat the wok or skillet with the oil. When hot, stir-fry the ginger and scallion over medium heat for 30 seconds. Add the crab meat, stir and mix. Sprinkle with salt and pepper and add the remaining stock and sherry or white wine. Stir-fry over high heat for 30 seconds. Spoon over the cabbage in the dish.

Honey Garlic-Shrimp

[SERVES 4]

1½ lb. large, raw shrimp	I egg
3 cloves garlic, crushed	⅔ cup milk and water
juice of 2 lemons	vegetable oil for deep-frying
2 tsp. sugar	2 tbsp. honey
I tbsp. soy sauce	I-inch fresh ginger root,
2 tbsp. olive oil	grated
freshly ground black pepper	2tsp cornstarch
I cup all-purpose flour	I tbsp. sesame seeds
2 pinches of salt	

1 Shell the shrimp and cut deeply along the back of each, removing the main vein.

2 Combine the crushed garlic, lemon juice, sugar, soy sauce, half the oil and a good shake of black pepper. Pour over the shrimp and leave to marinate in a cool place for 2–4 hours.

3 Make the batter by sifting together the flour and salt. Add the egg, the remaining oil and finally the milk and water mixture, a little at a time, until the batter will coat the back of a spoon. Store in the refrigerator.

4 Drain the shrimp and reserve the marinade. Dip each shrimp in the batter and deep-fry for 1½ minutes in very hot fat until crisp and golden. Drain the shrimp on paper towels and keep warm in a serving dish.

5 Heat the remaining marinade with the honey, grated ginger and cornstarch. Stir constantly until the sauce thickens. Allow to simmer, still stirring, for several minutes.

6 Pour the sauce over the shrimp and turn them gently in it until well coated. Sprinkle with the sesame seeds and serve immediately.

Ginger-Shrimp Stir-fry

[SERVES 2]

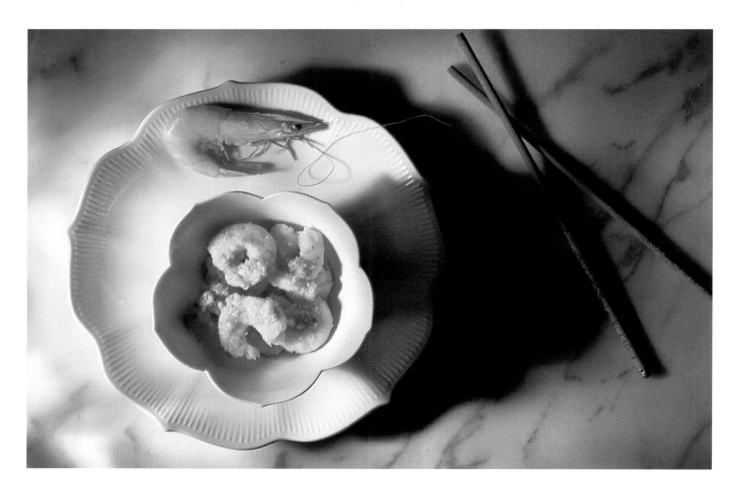

¾ lb. large shrimp	**1 tbsp. dry sherry**
1½-inch fresh ginger root,	**1 tbsp. oil**
peeled and grated	**pinch of Chinese 5-spice powder**
juice of 1 lime	**salt, pepper and sugar to taste**

1 Shell and devein the shrimp and put them into a strong plastic bag. Add the ginger, lime juice and sherry and tie the top of the bag securely. Put it into a bowl in case of leaks and leave it to marinate in a cool place (not the refrigerator) for 2–4 hours.

2 Heat the oil in a wok or a large, heavy skillet. Drain the shrimp and stir-fry them for 2–3 minutes, depending on size, until just firm.

3 Add the Chinese 5-spice powder and marinade and season to taste.

4 Warm the sauce through and serve immediately.

Shrimp Quiche with Poppy Seeds

[SERVES 6]

1½ cups all-purpose flour	**FOR THE FILLING**
good pinch of salt	3 eggs, lightly beaten
1 tsp. paprika	¾ cup cream cheese
pinch of cayenne	1 cup light cream
½ cup butter, softened	½ lb. frozen shrimps, thawed
1 egg yolk	3 blades of mace, broken into
3–4 tbsp. poppy seeds	small pieces
	salt and white pepper to taste

1 Preheat the oven to 425°F. Sift together the flour, salt, paprika and cayenne and cut in the butter until the mixture resembles fine crumbs. Add the egg yolk and poppy seeds, and press the dough – it will be too fragile to roll – into a 9-inch quiche pan.

2 Line the dough with foil, fill with dried beans and bake for about 20 minutes. Remove the foil and beans and leave to cool. Reduce the oven heat to 350°F.

3 For the filling, blend the eggs into the cream cheese. Stir in the cream, shrimp and mace and season to taste.

4 Pour this mixture into the pastry case and bake for 25 minutes or so, until just set but still slightly creamy. Serve warm.

Shrimp Salad

[SERVES 4]

¼ lb. jumbo shrimp	snipped fresh chives
1 avocado	chopped fresh parsley
2 oranges	French dressing (see right)
¼ lb. snow peas, cooked	salt and freshly ground
¼ lb. cauliflower flowerets,	black pepper
cooked	

1 Pick over and shell the shrimp. Remove the black vein, using a small sharp knife.

2 Peel, stone and slice the avocado. Peel the oranges, as you would an apple, leaving no pith on the flesh, then cut into segments.

3 Toss all the ingredients together in the French dressing. Season well. Serve on individual plates and hand whole-wheat bread and butter separately.

Basic French Dressing

Basic French dressing can be made and refrigerated. Small quantities can then be flavored as required. Always use a good-quality wine vinegar. There are many varieties of flavored vinegars readily available and they should be used in slightly smaller proportions than in the recipe.

3 parts oil	salt and pepper
1 part wine vinegar	

1 Put all the ingredients together in a screw-topped jar. Before using shake until well emulsified.

Note 1 *This dressing can be flavored with crushed garlic, mustard, sugar, chopped fresh herbs and so on, as desired. With walnut or hazelnut oil use 5 parts oil to 1 part vinegar; with olive oil (only use virgin oil) use 4 parts oil to 1 part vinegar or lemon juice; with other salad oils use proportions as in the recipe. Do not use any strongly flavored oil, such as sesame, coconut, except in small quantities.*

Note 2 *If kept refrigerated the dressing will more easily form an emulsion when shaken or beaten, and has a slightly thicker consistency. If over-chilled, however, the oil will have an unpleasantly stringy texture and will need gentle warming in the jar under hot water.*

Seafood and Pasta Salad

[SERVES 4]

I lb. green and white fettucine	¼ lb. squid
3 oz. smoked salmon	I ¼ cups mussels, live
¼ lb. cooked shelled shrimp	I small onion, chopped
lemon juice	¼ cup white wine
salt and freshly ground	French Dressing (see page 143)
black pepper	I tbsp. chopped fresh dill
	½ cup sour cream

I Cook the pasta in plenty of boiling salted water, to which 2 tbsp. oil has been added, until just tender. Drain well, rinse off any excess starch with plenty of boiling water and leave spread out to drain and cool. (Do not rinse in cold water as this prevents the pasta "steaming off" and drying.)

2 Chop the smoked salmon. Sprinkle the shrimp with lemon juice and pepper. Set aside.

3 Clean and slice the squid. Wash the mussels, scrub well and remove the threadlike "beards" hanging from them. Throw away any mussels which remain open when tapped.

4 Place the squid in a saucepan with the onion and wine. Cover with a lid and poach very gently for 1 minute (more will toughen the flesh). Remove with a slotted spoon.

5 Put the mussels into the wine in the pan. Cover and cook gently for about 5 minutes or until all the shells have opened. Throw away any mussels that have not opened. Drain the mussels but cover them with a damp dish towel to prevent drying out as they steam dry.

6 Mix together the French Dressing, dill and sour cream. Add it to the pasta, squid, smoked salmon and shrimp. Mix well and check the seasoning. Transfer to a clean dish and put the mussels on top. (Remove the mussels from their shells if they are to be eaten at a stand-up party with a fork. Otherwise leave them in their shells and arrange them on top of the salad where they will look most attractive unshelled.)

Jumbo Shrimp in Garlic Butter

[SERVES 4]

Whole-wheat bread and lots of napkins are needed to enjoy these to the full – eat them with your fingers

I ½ lb. live jumbo shrimp	FOR THE GARNISH
½ cup garlic butter	lemon wedges
(made with unsalted butter)	parsley sprigs

I Boil some water and salt in a large pan. Plunge the shrimp in the water. Bring back to a boil and cook for 1 minute.

2 Drain the shrimp and toss in hot garlic butter for 2–3 minutes. Serve with lemon wedges and parsley.

Quick-fried Crystal Shrimp

[SERVES 4–5]

¾ lb. large shrimp, fresh or frozen, unshelled	2 slices fresh ginger root, finely chopped
I tsp. salt	2 scallions, finely chopped
I ½ tbsp. cornstarch	3–4 tbsp. green peas (optional)
I egg white	2½ tbsp. fish stock (see page 18)
½ tsp. sugar	I ½ tbsp. dry sherry or white wine
pepper to taste	
⅔ cup vegetable oil	

I Shell the shrimp. Wash in salted water, then rinse under running cold water and drain well. Place in a bowl. Add salt, cornstarch, egg white, sugar, pepper and ½ tsp. vegetable oil. Mix well.

2 Heat the oil in a wok or deep skillet. When hot, add the shrimp, stir around and fry over medium heat for 1¾ minutes. Remove and drain. Pour away the oil to use for other purposes, leaving only 1–1½ tbsp. Reheat the wok or pan. When hot, stir-fry the ginger, scallion and peas over high heat for 15 seconds. Add the stock and sherry or wine. As the sauce boils, return the shrimp and adjust the seasoning. Fry for 1 minute.

Jumbo Shrimp in Garlic Butter

Seafood Cassolette

[SERVES 4]

This recipe transforms a traditional meat cassoulet, with its long slow cooking and hearty ingredients, into a light, quickly cooked fish cassolette.

2 tbsp. butter
2 tbsp. finely chopped shallots
4 cooked crayfish, shelled
4 scallops
¼ lb. sole fillets,
cut into strips
¼ lb. cooked shelled shrimp
12 fresh basil leaves, thinly sliced
¾ cup dry white wine
¾ cup fish stock

½ cup heavy cream
2 tbsp. Red Shellfish Butter
(see page 147), diced
salt and freshly ground
white pepper

FOR THE GARNISH
tomato concassé
crayfish
sprigs of dill

1 Melt the butter in a skillet and add the shallots. Cover and cook over a moderate heat, shaking the pan occasionally, until soft. Add the crayfish and cook for 2 minutes.

2 Remove the scallops from their shells, separate the bodies from the corals and cut the bodies in half. Add to the pan with the sole,

shrimp, basil, wine and stock and cook gently for 2 minutes. Remove the fish with a slotted spoon and keep warm.

3 Reduce the liquid by three-quarters, then stir in the cream and simmer until slightly thickened. Reduce the heat to very low and gradually beat in the Red Shellfish Butter, making sure that each piece is completely incorporated before adding the next. Season.

4 Divide the fish between 4 warmed plates, arranging them attractively, then spoon the sauce over. Garnish with the concassé tomatoes, crayfish and sprigs of dill.

Broiled Scampi

[SERVES 4]

Scampi is the Italian for langoustine. The creatures are the same size as large Mediterranean shrimp, but are distinguished from them by their prominent, lobster-like claws. They can be bought live or frozen uncooked. On no account buy cooked ones: it does not improve the flavor to cook fish twice.

24 large scampi
⅔ cup olive oil
juice of I lemon

3 tbsp. freshly grated Parmesan
cheese
½ cup fresh bread crumbs
kosher salt

1 Cut the scampi in half lengthwise, leaving a thin strip of shell at the back so the 2 pieces remain just attached.

2 Combine half the oil and the lemon juice and brush each fish with the mixture. Combine the cheese and the bread crumbs and sprinkle over the exposed flesh. Sprinkle the fish with the remaining oil and dot with kosher salt.

3 Preheat the broiler to maximum and broil until the cheese forms a light brown crust. Serve instantly.

Lime Shrimp

[SERVES 6]

Light on fat and heavy on flavor, this is an easy and delicious barbecue recipe.

½ cup peanut oil
¼ cup freshly squeezed lime juice
4 cloves garlic, finely chopped
2 tbsp. chopped fresh cilantro
½ tsp. chili pepper flakes

½ tsp. salt
¼ tsp. black pepper
1 ½ lb. medium shrimp, shelled and deveined

1 In a glass or other non-reactive bowl, mix together all the ingredients, except the shrimp until well combined. Add the shrimp, turning to make sure each is thoroughly coated, then refrigerate for several hours, turning once or twice. If you are using wooden skewers, soak the skewers in water for at least 1 hour while the shrimp are marinating. This helps prevent the skewers burning.

2 Thread the shrimp on the skewers; they should not touch each other. When the coals have stopped flaming, place the skewers on the broiler, directly over the coals. Cook just until the shrimp are opaque and tightly curled, 2–3 minutes a side, turning once. Do not overcook or the shrimp will toughen.

Shrimp Creole

[SERVES 6]

Whenever possible, start with whole shrimp and use the heads and shells to make a rich seafood stock for this dish. You can make the sauce ahead of time, then reheat and add the shrimp just before serving. This recipe is only mildly spicy, so add more cayenne or hot-pepper sauce if you want a fiery dish.

2 tbsp. vegetable oil
1 ½ cups chopped onion
1 large green pepper, chopped
2 celery sticks, chopped
3 garlic cloves, finely chopped
3 cups seeded and chopped
   fresh tomatoes
1 cup tomato sauce
½ cup dry red wine or fish stock
   (see page 18)
1 ½ cups fish stock
   (see page 18)
1 tsp. salt
2 bay leaves

2 tbsp. chopped fresh parsley
1 tbsp. chopped fresh basil,
   or 1 tsp. dried
1 ½ tsp. fresh thyme,
   or ½ tsp. dried
½ tsp. black pepper
¼ tsp. cayenne
few drops of hot-pepper sauce
1 tbsp. freshly squeezed
   lemon juice
1 lb. medium shrimp,
   shelled and deveined
6 scallions, chopped
2 cups cooked rice, to serve

1 In a large saucepan, heat the oil. Sauté ¾ cup onions until golden. Add the remaining onions, green pepper, celery and garlic, and sauté until the vegetables are limp, about 5 minutes.

2 Add the tomatoes, tomato sauce, wine, stock, seasonings, hot-pepper sauce and lemon juice. Bring to a boil, stir well, then reduce the heat and simmer for 30 minutes.

3 Just before serving, add the shrimp and scallions and cook just until the shrimp are opaque and tightly curled, 5–7 minutes. Serve over rice.

Red Shellfish Butter

½ cup red shellfish shells,
   crushed
10 tbsp. butter, softened

salt
cayenne pepper
brandy

1 Beat the shells and butter together, then heat very gently, stirring constantly, until a froth rises to the surface. Very carefully pour off the clear liquid beneath the froth into a strainer lined with cheese cloth. Leave to set in a cool place then beat in a little salt, cayenne and brandy.

Boiled Shrimp

[MAKES 450g/1 lb]

Here is a basic recipe for cooking shrimp that are to be eaten cold with a dip, rémoulade sauce or in a salad. Whether you shell them before you cook them is a matter of personal preference. If you like, you can also use wine or beer as the cooking liquid, and you can increase the amount of chili flakes if you like your shrimp spicy.

2½ quarts water
2 carrots, sliced
1 onion, sliced
2 cloves garlic, crushed
1 bay leaf
parsley sprigs

1 tsp. salt
1 tbsp. whole mustard seed
1 tsp. black pepper
¼ tsp. dried chili flakes
1 lemon, sliced
1 lb. shrimp

1 Bring the water to a boil in a large saucepan. Add the carrots, onion, garlic, bay leaf and parsley and continue boiling for 10 minutes to release the vegetables' flavors into the cooking liquid. Add the spices and lemon and boil for another 2 minutes.

2 Add the shrimp and boil just until the shrimp are opaque and tightly curled, 2–3 minutes. Do not overcook or the shrimp will become tough. Drain and refrigerate, or put on ice.

Crayfish Pie

[SERVES 6–8]

Paprika colors the rich-and-creamy filling pink in this recipe. If you can find crayfish tails already peeled and cooked, buy them – you are in for a lot of work if you have to cook and clean enough whole crayfish to produce enough tail meat for this recipe.

¼ cup lard
¼ cup all-purpose flour
I cup chopped onion
I large celery stick, chopped
½ large green pepper, chopped
2 garlic cloves, finely chopped
2 tbsp. chopped fresh parsley
½ cup fish stock
(see page 18), or clam juice
¼ cup light cream
I tsp. paprika
¾ tsp. fresh thyme, or ¼ tsp. dried

I ½ tsp. chopped fresh basil,
or ½ tsp. dried
¼ tsp. black pepper
¼ tsp. cayenne
large pinch of white pepper
I tsp. salt
2 tsp. freshly squeezed
lemon juice
I ½ lb. crayfish tails,
shelled and cooked
6 scallions, chopped
piecrust dough for 2-crust pie

1 In a heavy saucepan, make a peanut-butter-colored roux of lard and flour. Remove from the heat, add the vegetables, garlic and parsley. Return to the heat and cook until the vegetables are wilted, about 5 minutes.

2 In another pan, heat the seafood stock and light cream to a slow boil. Beat in the roux, 1 large spoonful at a time, beating after each addition. Add the seasonings and lemon juice and bring to a boil, then reduce the heat and simmer for 20 minutes. Add the crayfish tails and scallions, Taste and adjust the seasonings, then leave to cool to lukewarm.

3 Preheat the oven to 375°F. Roll out the dough and line a deep, oval 9-inch baking dish with half of it, sprinkling a little flour over the bottom to prevent sogginess. Add the filling and top with the second crust. Trim and seal the edges, pinching into a fluted edge. Bake until the crust is golden brown, about 30 minutes. Leave to cool for about 10 minutes before serving.

Crayfish Étouffée

[SERVES 4-6]

Étouffée means "smothered" in French, and here a rich, spicy roux-based
sauce smothers the crayfish. The sauce can be made ahead of time then
reheated and the crayfish added just before serving.

½ cup lard
½ cup all-purpose flour
1½ cups chopped onion
I large green pepper, chopped
I large celery stick, chopped
4 cloves garlic, finely chopped
4 medium tomatoes,
seeded and chopped
1½ cups chopped fresh parsley
2 cups fish stock
(see page 18)

½ tsp. cayenne
½ tsp. black pepper
I tsp. salt
1½ tsp. black pepper
1½ tsp. fresh thyme,
or ½ tsp. dried
1½ lb. crayfish tails,
shelled and cooked
8 scallions, chopped
2 cups cooked rice
to serve

I In a heavy saucepan, make a mahogany-colored roux of the lard and flour. Remove from the heat and stir in the vegetables and parsley. Return to the heat and cook until the vegetables are limp, about 5 minutes.

2 In a large saucepan, bring the seafood stock to a slow boil. Add the roux and vegetables, 1 spoonful at a time, beating after each addition until the mixture is smooth. Add the seasoning. Reduce the heat and simmer for 30 minutes.

3 Add the crayfish tails and simmer until the crayfish is heated through, about 5 minutes. Just before serving, stir in the scallions. Serve over rice.

Moules au Gratin

[SERVES 2]

pinch of saffron threads
¼ cup hot water
2 lb. uncooked mussels in their
shells
¼ cup white wine
½ small onion, chopped
½ bay leaf

2 tbsp. butter
2 tbsp. all-purpose flour
⅔ cup hot milk
salt and white pepper to taste
I tbsp. fresh white bread crumbs
I tbsp. grated Parmesan cheese

I Infuse the saffron threads in the hot water for 30 minutes.

2 Scrub the mussels well and remove the "beards." Discard any that are the slightest bit open.

3 Put the mussels in a large saucepan with the saffron infusion, wine, onion and bay leaf, and simmer, covered, until the mussels open.

4 Take the pan off the heat, strain off the liquid and reserve. Discard any mussels that are closed. Remove the mussels from their shells.

5 Preheat the oven to 400°F. Melt three-quarters of the butter. Add the flour and cook for a moment or two. Gradually stir in the hot milk and ⅔ cup of the mussel liquid. Season and simmer for 4 minutes.

6 Off the heat, add the shelled mussels and divide the mixture between 2 individual gratin dishes.

7 Sprinkle with the bread crumbs and Parmesan. Dot with the remaining butter and bake in a preheated oven for 10 minutes or so, until the topping is lightly browned. Serve immediately.

Crayfish Étouffée

Crayfish and Mushroom Ragout

[SERVES 4]

16 fresh crayfish
court bouillon (see page 19)
1 tbsp. butter, diced
½ tbsp. finely chopped shallots
⅓ cup sliced ceps
¼ tsp. finely chopped thyme
½ clove of garlic, finely chopped
salt and freshly ground
white pepper

1 tbsp. Pernod
6 tbsp. dry white wine
⅔ cup heavy cream

FOR THE GARNISH
sprigs of chervil
slices of truffle

1 Poach the crayfish in the court bouillon for about 10 minutes until bright red. Remove and keep warm. Keep the court bouillon warm.

2 Melt the butter in a skillet. Add the shallots, ceps, thyme, garlic and seasoning and cook for 2–3 minutes. Stir in the Pernod and wine and reduce by half. Stir in the cream. Season.

3 Remove the crayfish from their shells. Bring the court bouillon to just below simmering point. Add the crayfish and heat for 30 seconds.

4 Transfer the crayfish to 4 warmed plates with a slotted spoon. Pour the sauce over. Garnish with chervil and slices of truffle.

Stuffed Mussels

[SERVES 4–6]

48 large mussels
⅔ cup white wine and water,
mixed
I cup unsalted butter

10 cloves garlic, crushed
2 cups fresh bread crumbs
lemon wedges

I Debeard and scrub the mussels. Throw away any mussels that remain open when tapped. Steam open the mussels in a little white wine and water. Drain and take off the top shell.

2 Soften the butter a little with your hands. Add the crushed garlic cloves and work the bread crumbs into the garlic butter.

3 Add a knob of stuffing to each mussel and put under a hot broiler.

4 Serve very hot with lemon wedges and crusty French bread.

Seafood
Jambalaya

Seafood Jambalaya

[SERVES 6–8]

The Cajun dish jambalaya is traditionally made with ham, but it's not a necessity. You may add 4–8 oz. chopped ham back in, if you desire.

2 tbsp. vegetable oil
I onion, chopped
I green bell pepper, chopped
2 celery sticks, chopped
3 cloves garlic, finely chopped
3 large tomatoes,
seeded and chopped
I × 8 oz. can tomato sauce
I cup fish stock
(see page 18)
¼ cup fresh parsley, chopped

2 bay leaves
I tbsp. fresh thyme or I tsp. dried
I tsp. salt
¼ tsp. black pepper
½ tsp. cayenne
large pinch of white pepper
2 lb. fresh shrimp, crab meat,
crayfish or oysters, or any
combination, prepared
½ cup spring onions, chopped
I lb. cooked rice to serve

I Heat the oil in a deep skillet or casserole. Sauté the onion, bell pepper, celery, and garlic until the vegetables are limp, about 5 minutes. Add the tomatoes, tomato sauce, stock, parsley, and seasonings, and simmer gently until the tomatoes are cooked down and some of the liquids have reduced. Taste and adjust the seasonings.

2 Add the seafood. (If using oysters, cut into bite-sized pieces and add in the last 2–3 minutes of cooking.) Simmer just until the shrimp are opaque and tightly curled, 5–7 minutes. Just before serving, mix in the spring onions. Serve over rice.

Note *If the rice is not cooked with salt, you will need additional salt in the jambalaya.*

Scallops with Mussel Packages

[SERVES 4]

½ cup dry white wine
16 mussels
16 spinach leaves
salt and freshly ground
white pepper
28 small scallops

FOR THE SAUCE
½ cup butter, diced
2 lb. shells from cooked
shrimp, crushed

½ lb. mixed chopped carrots
and leeks and diced celery
I tsp. tomato paste
2 tbsp. cognac
I cup dry white wine
15 oz. fish stock
¼ pt. heavy cream
salt and freshly ground
white pepper

I For the sauce, heat the butter, and add the shrimp shells and vegetables, and cook over a low heat for about 5 minutes, stirring occasionally. Stir in the paste and cognac and ignite with a taper. Stir in the wine and boil until nearly all the liquid has evaporated. Stir in the stock and reduce until syrupy. Stir in the cream and seasoning, and simmer for about 3 minutes. Pass through a strainer, pressing down well to extract as much liquid as possible. Keep warm over a low heat.

2 Heat the wine, add the mussels, and steam for a few seconds until they have only just opened. Remove them from their shells and drain well.

3 Blanch and refresh the spinach leaves and drain well. Spread them out and place a mussel in the center of each. Fold the leaves over to make neat packages, but leave one end open so part of the mussel shows. Place over a steamer to keep warm.

4 Reheat the wine with a little seasoning to just below simmering point. Remove the scallops from their shells, add to the wine, and poach for about 45 seconds each side.

5 Coat 4 warmed plates with sauce, arrange 4 spinach-wrapped mussels in the center of each one, and arrange 7 scallops round.

Mussel and Onion Stew

2 quarts mussels
⅔ cup dry white wine and water,
mixed
6 Spanish onions, sliced
¼ cup butter, or
4 tbsp. olive oil
4 shallots, chopped

6 cloves garlic
2 carrots, chopped
4 potatoes, peeled and sliced
I bouquet garni
chopped fresh parsley
black pepper

1 Scrub and debeard the mussels. Place them in a large saucepan with the white wine and some water. Cook on a high heat until the mussels are open – remember to discard any that remain firmly shut. Remove the mussels and strain the liquid.

2 In another pan, soften the onions in butter or olive oil. Add the shallots, garlic, carrots, potatoes, bouquet garni, parsley and the liquid from cooking the mussels. Season to taste with pepper. Simmer for about 1 hour.

3 Meanwhile, shell the mussels and reserve.

4 Take a ladleful of the vegetable broth from the pot, making sure you include some potatoes, then purée. Add to the rest of the vegetables again and put all the mussels into the pot. Simmer until the mussels are hot. (Do not boil as the mussels will get tough.)

5 Serve in deep bowls with wedges of garlic bread.

Gratinée of Scallops

[SERVES 6]

⅔ cup butter
1 small onion, very finely chopped
2 lb. scallops, out of the shells
and trimmed
1¼ cups dry white wine
2½ cups Béchamel Sauce
(see page 18)

½ tsp. dry mustard
4½ tbsp. dry vermouth
pinch of cayenne pepper
2 cups soft white bread crumbs
salt and pepper to taste

1 Preheat the oven to 400°F. Melt ¼ cup butter over a low heat. Add the onion and soften it in the butter. Add the trimmed scallops to the pan. Pour in the wine, bring to a boil, then simmer gently for 1 minute.

2 Remove the scallops from the broth and set aside. Boil the broth hard to reduce it to about one-quarter of the volume.

3 Slice the scallops and fold them into one-half of the Béchamel Sauce. Add the mustard, vermouth, cayenne, the reduced broth from the pan and salt and pepper to taste.

4 Spoon the mixture into 6 ovenproof dishes or 6 cleaned scallop shells. Coat with the rest of the Béchamel Sauce.

5 Melt the remaining butter and mix with the bread crumbs. Sprinkle the crumbs over each portion and bake for 12–15 minutes in a hot oven.

Scallops with Saffron Sauce

[SERVES 4]

16 large scallops
1½ tbsp. butter
2 tbsp. finely chopped shallots
salt and freshly ground pepper
⅔ cup medium-bodied dry
white wine
I cup fish stock
I cup heavy cream

several strands of saffron
dissolved in a little of the
white wine

FOR THE GARNISH
sprigs of dill
concassé tomatoes

1 Open the scallops. Separate the corals from the bodies and cut the bodies in half horizontally. Place on a cloth.

2 Heat the butter and add the shallots. Cover and cook over a low heat, shaking the pan occasionally, until soft.

3 Season the scallops, add the bodies to the pan, then cook over a low heat for 1 minute. Add the corals and cook for a further minute.

4 Remove the scallops with a slotted spoon, cover and keep warm.

5 Stir the wine into the pan and reduce to 2 tbsp. Stir in the stock and reduce to ¼ cup. Stir in the cream and dissolved saffron, and simmer until slightly thickened. Season.

6 Divide the sauce between the warmed plates. Arrange the scallop bodies and corals on top. Garnish with sprigs of dill and concassé tomatoes.

Scallops with Dill

[SERVES 4]

12 scallops
¼ cup butter
2 small leeks, cut into julienne
2 small carrots, cut into julienne
1 zucchini, cut into fine batons
⅔ cup fish stock
⅔ cup dry white wine
5 tbsp. heavy cream

sea salt and freshly ground
white pepper
2 tbsp. chopped fresh dill

FOR THE GARNISH
snow peas, cut into julienne, or
sprigs of dill

1 Remove the scallops from their shells. Reserve their liquid. Separate the corals and cut the bodies in half horizontally.

2 Melt half the butter in a large heavy pan. Add the vegetables and cook, covered, over a low heat for about 4 minutes, shaking the pan occasionally. Do not allow them to brown. Stir in the stock, scallop liquid and wine and bring to a boil. Reduce to about 5 tbsp., then stir in the cream and simmer for a few minutes until the sauce thickens slightly. Season lightly.

3 Melt the remaining butter. Add the scallops, a little salt and most of the dill. Cook gently for 1 minute, turn them over, add the corals and cook for a further minute – do not leave them to brown or toughen.

4 Tip a little of the scallop cooking liquid into the sauce and stir briefly to mix.

5 Meanwhile, blanch, refresh and drain the julienne of snow peas, if using.

6 Divide the sauce and vegetables between 4 warmed dishes and arrange the scallops and corals on top. Sprinkle with the remaining dill and garnish with julienne of snow peas or sprigs of dill.

Fried Squid

[SERVES 6]

4½ lb. small squid		2½ cups vegetable oil
1½ cups all-purpose flour		3 lemons
salt and freshly ground		
black pepper		

1 Clean the squid. Slice the body sacs into rings – 5 or 6 per body for small squid.

2 Heat the oil until it is almost smoking. Fry the squid in batches small enough not to produce a serious drop in the oil temperature. If in any doubt, start with just 2 or 3 and slowly work up.

3 Season the flour with salt and pepper. Dip the squid in the flour, one batch at a time so the coating does not become soggy, shake off the excess and fry until light brown – about 30–40 seconds if the temperature is right. Set each batch to drain on paper towels.

4 Check for salt once more when all is cooked and serve very hot, with the lemon cut in wedges.

Quick Fry of Three Sea Flavors

[SERVES 4–6]

If wine-lee paste is unavailable, substitute 1½ tbsp. dry sherry and
½ tbsp. brandy mixed with 1 tsp. cornstarch.

¼ lb. large shelled shrimp
6 medium scallops
3–4 oz. squid
1½ tsp. salt
pepper to taste
6 tbsp. vegetable oil
2 slices fresh ginger root,
shredded
1 medium fresh green chili,
seeded and shredded

2 scallions,
cut into ½-inch shreds
2 cloves garlic, finely chopped
1 carrot, thinly sliced
1 celery stick, thinly sliced
2 tbsp. fish stock (see page 18)
1 tbsp. light soy sauce
2 tbsp. Chinese wine-lee
paste
1 tsp. sesame oil

1 Cut each shrimp into 3 sections and the scallops in half. Clean the squid under running cold water and score with criss-cross cuts ½ inch apart, then cut into similar size pieces as the shrimp sections. Sprinkle on the salt, pepper and 1½ tsp. vegetable oil.

2 Heat 4 tbsp. of the oil in a wok or skillet. When hot, stir-fry the shrimp, scallops and squid over high heat for 1½ minutes. Remove with a slotted spoon.

3 Pour in the remaining oil. Reheat and add the ginger, chili, scallions, garlic, carrot and celery. Stir-fry quickly over high heat for 30 seconds, then pour in the stock, soy sauce and wine-lee paste. When boiling, return the "three sea flavors" and stir together for about 1 minute. Sprinkle over the sesame oil.

Oysters in Champagne Sauce

[SERVES 4]

⅔ cup Hollandaise Sauce
(see page 18)
2 shallots, finely chopped

7 tbsp. champagne
16 oysters on the half shell

1 Make the Hollandaise Sauce. Add the shallots and the champagne to the sauce.

2 Spoon a little of the sauce on each oyster. Bubble under the broiler for less than 2 minutes and serve.

Angels on Horseback

[SERVES 4]

12 oysters
12 slices of bacon

12 triangles of fried bread

1 Open the oysters and take out the flesh. Roll one slice of bacon around each oyster. Secure with a toothpick.

2 Cook under a hot broiler and serve on hot triangles of fried bread.

Oysters in Champagne Sauce

Sole with Oyster Packages

[SERVES 4]

I tbsp. finely chopped shallot
⅔ cup fish stock
I tbsp. dry vermouth
6 fillets of sole, skinned and cut
into strips
salt and freshly ground pepper
12 oysters
12 lettuce leaves

I small sprig of fresh thyme
⅔ cup heavy cream
I ½ tsp. white wine vinegar
I tbsp. butter, diced
I tsp. finely chopped, fresh chervil
12 diamond shapes of tomato
flesh, to garnish

I Simmer the shallot in the stock and vermouth for 3–4 minutes in a small, covered pan. Pour into a skillet that will hold the sole in a single layer. Lay the sole strips in the pan, season, cover with parchment and poach for about 1½ minutes until just opaque.

2 Carefully transfer to a warmed dish with a slotted spoon. Cover and keep warm.

3 Meanwhile, open the oysters. Blanch the lettuce leaves, drain well and dry on absorbent kitchen paper.

4 Add the oysters to the poaching liquid and poach for 30 seconds. Remove with a slotted spoon and wrap each oyster into a lettuce leaf, folding the leaf over to make a neat package.

5 Meanwhile, add the thyme to the liquid, then reduce to ¼ cup. Pour into a small saucepan, stir in the cream and simmer for 5 minutes. Pass through a strainer. Return to the heat, stir in the vinegar and reheat gently then, over a low heat. Gradually beat in the butter, making sure each piece is fully incorporated before adding the next. Stir in the chervil.

6 Spoon the sauce over 4 warmed plates. Arrange the strips of sole and the oyster packages in the sauce. Place a diamond of tomato on each parcel.

Braised Squid with a Parsley Stuffing

[SERVES 6]

12 squid (about 3¼ inches long)
2 tbsp. finely chopped fresh
parsley
2 cloves garlic, crushed
3 tbsp. freshly grated
Parmesan cheese
½ cup fresh bread crumbs
2 anchovy fillets

I egg
6 tbsp. olive oil
½ lb. fresh or canned
plum tomatoes
⅔ cup dry white wine
I chili pepper
salt to taste

I Clean the squid and finely chop the tentacles.

2 Combine the parsley, the garlic, the Parmesan cheese and the bread crumbs. Mash and mix in the anchovy fillets.

3 Beat the egg and mix it with the bread mixture. Add about half the oil and the tentacles of the squid. Now push the mixture into the squid bodies, stopping about two-thirds of the way down. (The squid will shrink as it cooks and thus push the stuffing down to the end.)

4 Heat the rest of the oil in a pan large enough to hold all the fish in one layer. Roughly chop the tomatoes and add them to the oil with the wine and the whole chili.

5 Bring the tomatoes and wine to a boil, then turn the heat to a very low simmer. Add the squid and seal the pan tightly. Cook for about 30 minutes, until a fork will easily pierce the squid. Season the sauce and wait, if you like – this dish may be served hot, cold or in between.

Paella

[SERVES 4]

1 tbsp. olive oil	6 oz. shelled shrimp, plus a
1 onion, finely sliced	few in their shells for garnish
1 clove garlic, crushed	1 cup chopped cooked chicken
1⅓ cups long-grain rice	1 cup chopped cooked ham
a few strands of saffron	2½ cups mussels,
2½ cups chicken stock, boiling	scrubbed and rinsed
salt and freshly ground	1¼ cups clams,
black pepper	thoroughly rinsed
1 cup peas	7 tbsp. dry white wine

1 Put the oil in a large microwave-safe pot and cook on Full for 30 seconds. Stir in the onion and garlic and cook on Full for 2 minutes. Stir in the rice and saffron. Pour over the boiling stock, add seasoning, cover and cook on Full for 8 minutes.

2 Stir in the peas, shrimp, chicken and ham. Cover and cook on Full for 4 minutes. Leave the pot to stand, covered, while you cook the mussels and clams.

3 Discard any open mussels. Put the mussels and clams in a large pot and pour the wine over. Cook on Full for about 3 minutes, until the shells have opened. Discard any shells that remain closed.

4 Arrange the paella on a heated serving plate. Take some of the mussels and clams out of their shells and add to the rice. Garnish the dish with the remaining mussels, clams and shrimp.

Squid with Beets

[SERVES 4]

1 lb. small squid
1 tbsp. olive oil
1 small onion, chopped
1 clove garlic, crushed
1 celery stick, finely chopped
2 cooked beets, chopped

3 tbsp. dry white wine
1 tbsp. tomato paste
salt and freshly ground
black pepper
celery tips

1 First clean the squid. Remove the eyes, mouth, ink sac, "nib" and outer membrane. Wash the squid well, then slice body and tentacles.

2 Put the olive oil in a microwave-safe pot and cook on Full for 30 seconds. Stir in the onion and garlic and cook on Full for 2 minutes.

3 Add the celery, beets and squid. Mix the white wine and tomato paste and pour over the squid. Cover and cook for 8 minutes, or until the squid is tender.

4 Season with salt and pepper and serve garnished with celery tips.

Shrimp and Zucchini

in Tomato Sauce

[SERVES 4]

1 tbsp. oil
2 shallots, chopped
4 baby zucchini, sliced
14-oz. can tomatoes, strained

14 oz. shelled shrimp
freshly chopped basil
salt and freshly ground
black pepper

1 Put the oil in a microwave-safe bowl and cook on Full for 30 seconds. Add the shallots and zucchini and cook on Full for 3 minutes.

2 Stir in the strained tomatoes and the shrimp and cook, covered with vented plastic wrap, for 5 minutes, until hot through.

3 Sprinkle with plenty of basil and season to taste with salt and pepper. Serve with rice.

Mussel Salad

[SERVES 4]

1 tbsp. butter
1 small onion, chopped
1 lb. mussels, well scrubbed
2 tbsp. lemon juice
2 tbsp. dry white wine
4 celery sticks, sliced
1 cup cooked green beans
cut into bite-sized pieces

1 red pepper,
cut into julienne strips
1½ cups sliced cooked potatoes
2 tbsp. mayonnaise
chopped fresh parsley
salt and freshly ground
black pepper

1 Put the butter in a deep microwave-safe pot and cook on Full for 30 seconds. Add the onion and cook on Full for 2 minutes.

2 Put in the mussels (discarding any that are broken or open), pour in the lemon juice and white wine and cook on Full, covered, for 3–4 minutes, until the mussels have opened.

3 Discard any closed shells. Allow the mussels to cool, then remove them from their shells.

4 Mix the mussels in a large bowl with the celery, green beans, red pepper and potatoes. Stir the mayonnaise into the cooking liquid and onion and pour over the salad.

5 Add chopped parsley and seasoning, mix well and serve.

Squid with Beetroot

Index